The Isles of Shoals in the Age of Sail

Schooner fishing for cod. *Drawing by H.W. Elliott and Captain J.W. Collins. Courtesy of the National Oceanic and Atmospheric Administration.*

C H Elliott
Collins

The Isles of Shoals in the Age of Sail

A Brief History

Russell M. Lawson, PhD

The History Press

Published by The History Press
Charleston, SC 29403
www.historypress.net

Cover image: Detail from *Isles of Shoals* by Frederick Childe Hassam. *Courtesy of Minneapolis Institute of Arts, Gift of the Martin B. Koon Memorial Collection.*

First published 2007

Manufactured in the United States

ISBN 978.1.59629.203.1

Library of Congress Cataloging-in-Publication Data

Lawson, Russell M., 1957-
The Isles of Shoals in the age of sail : a brief history / Russell M. Lawson.
p. cm.
Includes bibliographical references.
ISBN 978-1-59629-203-1 (alk. paper)
1. Isles of Shoals (Me. and N.H.)--History. 2. Isles of Shoals (Me. and N.H.)--History, Naval. 3. Isles of Shoals (Me. and N.H.)--Biography. I. Title.
F42.I8L29 2007
974.1'95--dc22
2007021392

For Riley, David and Benjamin

Contents

Star Island. *Courtesy of Russell M. Lawson.*

On Star Island

High on the lichened ledges, like
A lonely sea-fowl on its perch,
Blown by the cold sea-winds it stands,
The quaint, forsaken Gosport church.
No sign is left of all the town
Except a few forgotten graves;
But to and fro the white sails go
Slowly across the glittering waves.
And summer idlers stray about,
With curious questions of the lost
And vanished village and its men
Whose boats by these same waves were tossed.
I wonder if the old church dreams
About its parish, and the days
The fisher-people came to hear
The preaching and the songs of praise.
Rough-handed, browned with sun and wind,
Heedless of fashion or of creed,
They listened to the parson's words—
Their pilot heavenward indeed.
Their eyes on week-days sought the church,
Their surest landmark, and the guide
That led them home from far at sea,
Until they anchored safe beside.
The harbor-wall still braves the storm
With its resistless strength of stone.
Now busy fishers all are gone,
The church is standing here alone.
I know the blue sea covers some,
And others in the rocky ground
Found narrow lodgings for their bones.
God grant their rest is sweet and sound!
I saw the worn rope idle hang
Beside me in the belfry brown.
I gave the bell a solemn toll:
I rang the knell for Gosport town.

Sarah Orne Jewett

Chapter 1

Smith's Isles

The wind rarely ceases. It is always present, save on those dreary days when the fog rolls in from the west, a massive wall of gray that slowly envelops and stills the movement of the wind. The only sound is the recurrent breaking of the sea against the rocks, like an endless battering against a fortress that will always stand. The sea attacks in all directions, never retreating, never growing still, always heaving and churning in endless movement. Life assumes the same regularity and constancy. Flora and fauna fill the Isles of Shoals with life and beauty; the natural experiences of the islands are the same year in and out, constant repetition being the way of nature. Sea creatures feed in the waters surrounding the Isles. Seals sun themselves on the ubiquitous rocks, and sometimes curiously pop their heads above water as if trying to get their bearings. Leviathans of the deep, sharks and whales, appear at times as well, pursuing the fish that seek shelter amid the shoals in and about the islands. Land creatures are few on the Isles, the most prominent being the smooth green snake, a small thin reptile, one to two feet long, nonpoisonous and non-threatening. Small, indistinct yet hardy cedars, crippled by the wind, grow on various Isles; Native Americans and European Americans used the wood of the red cedar and white cedar for boats, canoes and building materials. Huckleberry and bayberry shrubs grow from the interstices of the rocky landscape, producing berries on which birds feed. The white flowers of the cherry become the ripe fruit of summer. The bright yellow flowers of the St. John's wort peek from behind granite boulders. White-flowered sea milkwort and beautiful scarlet pimpernel decorate the Isles on sunny days, the latter plant nicknamed the poor man's

Rocky shore and wildflowers at the Isles of Shoals. *Courtesy of Russell M. Lawson.*

weatherglass because the flowers close with the approach of storms. The purple and red flowers of the aster and morning glory grace the Isles during summer months. The bright scarlet velvet fruit of the staghorn sumac attracts birds and fowl large and small.

Year after year gulls return to nest on the same islands, soaring in from among the wispy clouds on a day of startling sunshine. The gulls chatter and look about in their odd way, awkwardly exploring the random rocks, weeds and flowers; fighting over crabs and fish; snooping about the rocky inlets and gorges where the sea rushes in and out; bringing and taking food. The gulls fight among themselves, the largest, the great black-backed gull, dominating the smaller herring gull. The two species nest together among shrubs and rocks, the larger gull feeding on small birds and ducks, eggs, shellfish and fish, the herring gull on fish and shellfish, sometimes dropping clams on rocky outcrops to break the shells and feed on the flesh. Other fowl compete for the resources of the Isles. Terns of various types, such as the common tern, breed on the rocky Isles and delight in the fish among the shoal water. White snowy owls in winter are well camouflaged among the white and gray rocks covered in snow and ice. The great cormorant and double-crested cormorant, or sea crow, dive and surface just offshore, finding herring and other edibles. The lonely call of the loon interrupts the late evening calm. Various ducks, especially the common eider, fly in to feed and mate, their ubiquitous presence on one Isle suggesting its less than prosaic name. Oldsquaw (the long-tailed duck) is a deep diver, feeding on fish and crustaceans. The sanderling winters among the Isles before returning to the Arctic in summer. Various species of sandpipers scamper across the few sandy spots and feed in rocky inlets.

The Sandpiper

Across the narrow beach we flit,
One little sandpiper and I,
And fast I gather, bit by bit,
The scattered driftwood bleached and dry.
The wild waves reach their hands for it,
The wild wind raves, the tide runs high,
As up and down the beach we flit,—
One little sandpiper and I.
Above our heads the sullen clouds
Scud black and swift across the sky;
Like silent ghosts in misty shrouds
Stand out the white lighthouses high.
Almost as far as eye can reach
I see the close-reefed vessels fly,

Double-crested cormorant. *Courtesy of the U.S. Fish and Wildlife Service Digital Library System.*

As fast we flit along the beach,—
One little sandpiper and I.
I watch him as he skims along,
Uttering his sweet and mournful cry.
He starts not at my fitful song,
Or flash of fluttering drapery.
He has no thought of any wrong;
He scans me with a fearless eye.
Stanch friends are we, well tried and strong,
The little sandpiper and I.
Comrade, where wilt thou be to-night
When the loosed storm breaks furiously?
My driftwood fire will burn so bright!
To what warm shelter canst thou fly?
I do not fear for thee, though wroth
The tempest rushes through the sky:
For are we not God's children both,
Thou, little sandpiper, and I?

Celia Thaxter

The first humans to visit the Isles are unknown. European legends posited a variety of mariners who might have made their way across the Atlantic to the Isles of the Blessed, the Fortunate Isles, Ogygia and the Hesperides—islands of imagination stoked by actual voyages of ancient and medieval sailors, the likes of Pytheas of Massilia, who claimed to have journeyed to Thule in the Atlantic, or the Carthaginians of North Africa who likewise claimed to have found massive islands many days' journey west across the sea. One legend has a medieval monk, St. Brendan, sailing west from Ireland in a curragh made of seal skin, discovering paradise before leaving (for some reason) and returning to his home. Legend gives way to history with the Vikings, the Norse sailors who voyaged at the beginning of the second millennium, AD, to a land they called Vinland. Archaeologists have found clear evidence of a Viking settlement at the northern tip of Newfoundland. It is not presently known whether or not other claims that they sailed along the coast of New England are factual. If the Vikings had sailed the cool waters of the Gulf of Maine, would they have found the Isles a lucky place to shelter in the middle of an Atlantic storm? Perhaps.

The first mention of the Isles in the literature of exploration occurs in Samuel de Champlain's account of his voyage along the New England coast in 1605. He laconically noted "three or four prominent islands" several miles east of the mainland. The first recorded exploration of the Isles was by Captain John Smith in June 1614. Long before the journeys of famed discoverers sailing on nationalist voyages for king and country, anonymous fishermen from fishing villages along the Atlantic coast of Portugal, France and England sailed the waters of the Gulf of Maine, harvesting from the cold brine a variety of marketable fish: cod, herring, mackerel, haddock. Farsighted men such as Champlain and Smith realized that the wealth of North America lay in such commodities. The competition between European monarchs, merchants and adventurers over North American fisheries, furs and forest products accelerated during the late sixteenth and early seventeenth centuries. Merchants, seamen and soldiers of the west English towns of Bristol and Plymouth sponsored numerous voyages along the coast of New England, hoping to beat the French in the race to establish successful colonies.

Captain John Smith was a leader in England's colonizing attempts along the New England coast from 1614 until his death in 1631. Smith was a soldier and self-made man who had, by his own account, single-handedly saved the Jamestown colony from failure from 1607 to 1609, when he returned to England after severely injuring himself. In 1614 he returned to America, this time accompanying a fishing and whaling voyage along the northern waters of Penobscot Bay. But "we found this Whale-fishing a costly conclusion; we saw many and spent much time in chasing them, but could not kill any." Seeking to yield success out of failure, Smith left behind the fishing for

Rocky forbidding shore of Isles of Shoals. *Courtesy of Russell M. Lawson.*

exploration, taking eight seamen with him in a small pinnace to explore the coast. They sailed along the coast of New England "seventie five leagues," from Penobscot Bay to Cape Cod. Along the way Smith took compass readings by which to map the coast, and kept extensive mental or written notes of the details of his experiences and observations. Smith discovered "at least fortie severall habitations" of Native Americans "upon the Sea Coast, and sounded about five and twentie excellent good Harbours." He explored hundreds of islands off the coast of Maine and Massachusetts. Inland, the country, he believed, was one "rather to affright, then delight…And how to describe a sore plaine spectacle of desolation, or more barren, I know not. Yet the Sea there is the strangest fishpond I ever saw; and those barren Isles so furnished with good woods, springs, fruits, fish, and foule, that it makes me thinke, though the Coast be rockie, and thus affrightable; the Vallies, Plaines, and interior parts may well (notwithstanding) be very fertile."

One June day the mariners spied islands in the distance and sought to explore them. Smith described them as "a heape together, none neere them." The irregular humps of rock rising from the water were brown, gray and white, forbidding and stark. The water thereabouts was shoal, demanding careful seamanship. They were largely barren and treeless. Breakwaters and windbreaks, the Isles were nevertheless daily, for eons, scoured by the wind over the surface and pounded by the waves upon the rocky shore. Years

The cold Atlantic surf. *Courtesy of Russell M. Lawson.*

later a disillusioned Smith in bitterness described the Isles as "a many of barren rocks, the most overgrown with such shrubs and sharp whins you can hardly pass them; without either grass or wood but three or four shrubby old cedars." Smith was adept at suggesting names for the places he explored—for example, he christened the region "New England." Strangely, of all the grand places, huge rivers and imposing shores, large hills and great harbors that Smith visited on his journeys about Chesapeake Bay and New England, he chose these scrubby Isles as his namesake.

Irony suffuses the history of the Isles of Shoals. That mere islands are thought beautiful is a wonder, being but patches of rock surrounded by the endless sea, seemingly helpless and insecure next to the massive swells that threaten to gobble them up. That people have chosen to live on a place so seemingly unlivable is another wonder. The precise political existence of the Isles has long been a matter of debate—islands so naturally united have for centuries been artificially divided between two different jurisdictions, Maine and New Hampshire. The irony of the history of the Isles begins with John Smith—an arrogant man, vain about his accomplishments, longing to be remembered—who chose to be remembered by a dozen tiny islands and rocks in a cold sea. So many were the great rivers and mountains Smith could have chosen. Yet even the name, Smith's Isles, did not last through his lifetime.

Why did Smith choose these islands as his namesake? He realized that the only people who could exist on such a remote and daunting place would be, like himself, those with persevering, hard, craggy personalities, people who had known trials and bitterness, self-made people willing to risk it all on a chance to create a successful community.

In subsequent years, Captain Smith argued that Smith's Isles would make a perfect place to establish a colony devoted to fishing. He dreamed of leading an expedition of mariners and fishermen to colonize Smith's Isles, to develop the fishing industry, and to cultivate the abilities of seamen to build and man small boats—shallops, pinnaces, barks and ketches. Smith made several failed attempts to return to the islands and was ostensibly granted title to Smith's Isles by the Council of New England in the 1620s. But by the time of his death in 1631, Smith's Isles had come to be known as the Isles of Shoals.

The fishermen who christened the islands knew nothing of the politics of grants, titles and the nomenclature of maps and books. They only knew that the Atlantic blew some mighty gales that tossed their fishing boats about in rising swells notwithstanding all of the will and strength that men could muster. They knew as well the dual nature of these islands, of their potential to serve as a safe harbor from the wind and waves at the same time that they loom in the dark, stormy night as the means of destruction and death. Even in the bright calm of day, the Isles demand careful navigation, as the depth of water ranges from less than a fathom to near twenty fathoms; ledges and rocks, some visible, others not, depending upon whether or not the tide is in or out, lie about, scarcely evident save for the swirling water and odd whitecaps that shoals make. Experience taught mariners to beware the Halfway Rocks that lie between Londoner's and Star Islands, ledges and rocks that lie off Duck Island in several directions, and submerged rocks between Cedar and Smuttynose. Cedar Ledge lies to the southeast of Cedar Island about a nautical quarter mile. Less that a mile to the south in apparently open water is Anderson's Ledge. White Island, too, has rocks and ledges guarding its approach. Whereas "Smith's Isles" served only to flatter one man's vanity, the "Isles of Shoals" served to warn sailors by its very name of the hazards surrounding these small islands in the sea. Parenthetically, some observers, such as Celia Langdon Thaxter, in *Among the Isles of Shoals*, argued that *shoals* could refer to "the 'shoaling,' or 'schooling,' of fish about [the Isles], which, in the mackerel and herring seasons, is remarkable."

The name preferred by fishermen and sailors, Isles of Shoals, found its way into documents of the 1620s. English mariner Phinehas Pratt, for example, who made port at the Isles in 1622, wrote that "we first arrived att Smithe's Islands, first soe called by Capt. Smith, att the time of his discovery of New England." But Pratt also noted that the Isles were "afterwards called 'Islands of Sholes.'" A year later, Captain Christopher Levett, a member of the

Mackerel schooner negotiating winds and waves. *Drawing by H.W. Elliott and Captain J.W. Collins. Courtesy of the National Oceanic and Atmospheric Administration.*

Council of New England, which had granted the captain six thousand acres in the New World, made port at the Isles. "The first place I set my foot upon in New England," Captain Levett wrote, "was the Isles of Shoulds"—at least "shoulds" was how the fishermen of the place pronounced it. Levett noted that the Isles had little vegetation, and an "indifferent" harbor good enough to moor half a dozen barks. The value of the Isles, he quickly saw, was in drying the catch from the deep. The fishermen had crowded the islands with their stages upon which to dry fish as a prelude to packing in barrels for export to Europe or the Caribbean. Levett noted another advantage of the Isles, which was the lack of Native Americans, who could hardly wish to reside in such an unlikely place. The fishing activity surrounding the Isles of Shoals at this early date is confirmed in John Winthrop's *Journal*, in which he noted that, sailing by the Isles in 1630, he saw a fishing shallop at port and five or six others engaged in coming or going to the fishing grounds.

The precise year that the first fishermen decided to make the Isles their permanent home is unknown. Nor is it known who they were, except that they were English, probably from West Country towns such as Plymouth and Bristol. It was a practical decision, saving on the time and expense (not to mention the danger) of yearly commutes from the British Isles to the Gulf of Maine. New settlements along the coast encouraged the establishment of a permanent, year-round fishing colony at the Isles. Newichawannock up the Piscataqua River and Pannaway at the river's mouth, the latter about six nautical miles to the northwest, could provide

Fishermen in a dory caught in a storm. *Drawing by H.W. Elliott and Capt. J.W. Collins. Courtesy of the National Oceanic and Atmospheric Administration.*

safe harbors should the Spanish or French attack the Isles. There were also the beginnings of a semblance of government, as the Isles of Shoals were part of a grant that King James I made to the Council of New England in 1620. Council membership included soldiers and landowners intent on creating great aristocratic manors in the fertile lands of New Hampshire and Maine. In 1621 and 1622, the council granted proprietary rights to settle and exploit northern New England to two soldiers and adventurers, Ferdinando Gorges and John Mason, who christened the land Laconia. According to a contemporary document, Pannaway, included in the grant to Gorges and Mason, included "Strawberry Bank, The Great House & Isles of Shooles." The proprietors had little success in establishing a thriving, successful province. The agents and employees they sent to Pannaway and Newichawannock in the Piscataqua Valley complained of lack of supplies and uncertain management. The fishermen at the Isles of Shoals, part of the proprietorship but receiving little direction, were therefore presented with the opportunity (or burden) of devising their own society and government, both of which were built around the sole occupation of the islands—fishing.

Fishermen from West Country English towns such as Bristol initially established temporary fishing camps on the Isles before the profitability of the cod fishery recommended a year-round presence. The Council of New England and the proprietors Gorges and Mason also sought a stable foundation for their holdings in New Hampshire and Maine by encouraging colonists to establish permanent homes in America. In 1634 the two proprietors divided

Whaleback lighthouse in mouth of Piscataqua. *From* Vignettes of Portsmouth.

their holdings, Gorges incorporating the northern Piscataqua Valley and Maine to the Saco River, and the northern Isles of Shoals (Duck, Malaga, Hog, Smuttynose, and Cedar), into his province of New Somersetshire; Mason meanwhile incorporated the southern Piscataqua Valley south to the Merrimack River, including Londoner's, White, and Star Islands, into his province of New Hampshire. After Mason's death in 1635, and with Gorges's age and inability to come to America to oversee his holdings, the towns of the Piscataqua in 1641 requested admittance as independent townships in the Massachusetts Bay colony. The inhabitants of the Isles of Shoals followed suit.

Early records suggest that Hog (Appledore) Island was the site of the first permanent settlement on the Isles. The advantages of Hog over the others were many, including a spring for water, soil for rudimentary gardens, grass for grazing livestock, and sufficient rocky indentations along the shore to moor fishing vessels. Besides, Hog, the largest of the islands, could best support extensive fishing operations. During the 1630s and early 1640s, the number of fishermen grew sufficiently large that the inhabitants built a brick meetinghouse and called a minister to preach. The stone foundations of the meetinghouse and fishermen's dwellings still existed when Nathaniel Hawthorne visited Hog Island in 1852. "There are several inclosures—" he wrote, "the largest perhaps thirty yards square—surrounded with a rough stone-wall of very mossy antiquity, built originally broad and strong, two or three large stones in width, and piled up breast-high or more, and taking

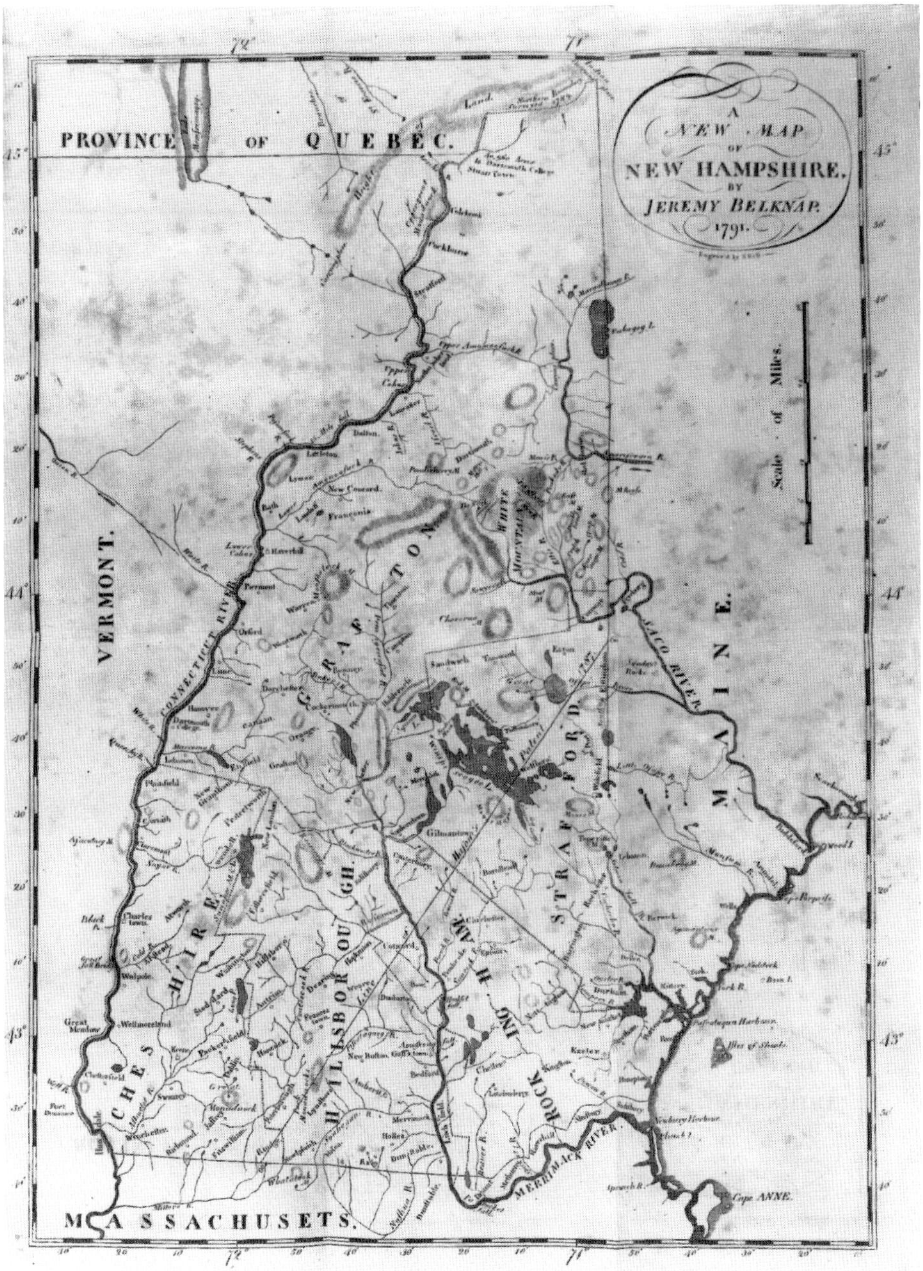

This detailed map of New Hampshire accompanied volume two of Jeremy Belknap's *History of New Hampshire*, published in 1791. *Courtesy of Dartmouth College Library.*

advantage of the extruding ledge to make it higher…Close by the inclosure is the hollow of an old cellar, with stones tumbled into it, but the layers of stone at the sides still to be traced, and bricks, broken or with rounded edges, scattered about, and perhaps pieces of lime."

Early fishermen christened the island Hog, perhaps because a ridge at the eastern side of the island had the appearance of a razorback. Contrary winds, heavy seas and stormy weather often kept small sailing boats tacking back and forth, making little headway, allowing sailors and fishermen the time to imagine what they would about the islands. The first use of "Hog Island" in print was during just such an occasion of contrary weather. In 1635, Richard Mather, father of Increase Mather and grandfather of Cotton Mather—the great Puritan historians and theologians—was aboard an English vessel bound for New England. The voyage had been a long one due to contrary winds. Upon reaching the New England coast, and crawling south from Monhegan Island toward Cape Ann, the captain, sailors and passengers enjoyed a gentle north wind that pushed them easily along toward the south. The sailors merrily fished for mackerel with great success. The evening of August 13, "our seamen desired to have ancred at Hog Iland, or ye Ile of Shoales, being 7 leagues short of Cape Anne…but ye wind being strong at south-southwest thay could not atteyne [their] purpose, and so were forced to lye off againe to sea all night." The next day, Friday the 14th of August, the wind continued from the south, which forced the captain to tack "too & againe, all day, one while west & by north towards Iles of Shoales, another while east-south-east to sea againe." By evening the wind finally relented to allow them "to ancre at ye Iles of Shoales, which are 7 or 8 Ilands & other great rockes; and there slept sweetely…till breake of day." Dawn, however, brought "forth a most terrible storme of raine and easterly wind, whereby wee were in as much danger as I thinke ever people were: for wee lost in that morning three great ancres & cables." The ship cast adrift among the rocky shore, the mariners' only hope was to make sail and allow the wind to drive them to safety. "But ye Lord let us see that our sayles could not save us neither, no more than our cables & ancres; for by ye force of ye wind & raine ye sayles were rent in sunder & split in pieces, as if they had beene but rotten ragges." In this extremity, "wee seemed to drive with full force of wind & rayne directly upon a mighty rocke standing out in sight above ye water, so that wee did but continually wayte, when wee should heare and feele ye dolefull rishing and crushing of ye ship upon ye rocke." All of a sudden the storm relented sufficiently to allow the ship to avoid the rocks and the sailors to rig temporary sails. Indeed a pleasant breeze came from the north, and the ship departed Hog Island southwest for Cape Ann.

At this time, in the 1630s, the islands became an important staging port for ships bound to and from England to load or unload cargos of fish for

Fishing schooner in distress. *Drawing by H.W. Elliott and Captain J.W. Collins. Courtesy of the National Oceanic and Atmospheric Administration.*

the outward voyage and marketable goods for the inward voyage. As a consequence, the Isles became an exit point to make sail for England and an entry point for news from abroad. The villain Thomas Morton, whose free-spirited activities made him anathema to Puritans, was arrested by the authorities of Plymouth Colony in 1628 and escorted by Captain Miles Standish to Hog Island, where he awaited an outgoing ship to take him to England. The fishermen who first resided at the Isles knew hard drink befitting hard work in dangerous conditions. Fishing year-round was only for the fit and strong, as "the hardships endured in taking the winter fish are inconceivable by all but eye witnesses." Groups of young men, sometimes three or four brothers, arrived at the Isles of Shoals in the 1630s and 1640s from the British Isles, intent on making a living in the New World. Examples include the Cutt brothers from Wales, who had great success as fishermen, merchants and landowners—Richard Cutt coming to own most if not all of Star Island, John Cutt becoming an economic and political leader of the Piscataqua Valley and Robert Cutt also enjoying economic success at the Shoals. The Seeley brothers, John, Richard and William, became political and economic leaders at Smuttynose Island. Likewise John, Roger and William Kelly were leaders of fishing and trade at Smuttynose.

That the different families of brothers lived as bachelors on the Isles, at least for a time, is illustrated by a law passed by the General Court of Massachusetts forbidding the presence of women at the Isles of Shoals. An increasing number of exceptions, however, led to the admittance of wives on the islands. A case in point was John Reynolds of Hog Island, who in 1647 broke the law by bringing a wife to the island. The General Court, responding to a petition from Shoalers that Reynolds be admonished for his crime, determined that "as for *the removal of his wife*, it is thought fit, if no further complaint come against her, *she may as yet enjoy the company of her husband*." The same year Henry Sherburne purchased land on Hog Island, whence he brought his wife, Rebecca Gibbins Sherburne, though soon after they relocated to the small island to the south, Malaga.

The first wives to live at the Isles were, like their husbands, coarse, profane, uneducated and illiterate. Fishwife Joan Forde in 1665, for example, called the Hog Island constable a "Hornheaded rogue and a Cowhead rogue," for which she received the punishment of "nine stripes given her at the post." In 1668 constable Roger Kelly charged fishwife Rebecca Downes with assault. Mary Kelly was brought to court several times, in 1669 for "abusing of her neighbours in an unseemly manner with badd words." Elizabeth Mannering in 1705 appeared in court for "abuse threaten and evill Intreat Elisha Kelley of Smuttynuse Island of the Isles of Shoals." The men frequently outdid the women in appearances in court, the violence of their actions, and the degree and gusto of their swearing. One violent row occurred a few days before Christmas in 1677. Three men, William Hilton, Samson White and John Andrews, went to the home of Roger Kelly on Smuttynose Island, having heard that Kelly and his crew of fishermen had accused the three of casting Kelly's fishing boat adrift while she lay moored at Smuttynose (Haley's) Cove. Kelly's men James Neale, John Ashe and Henry Harvey faced their opponents and repeated the accusation. A violent confrontation ensued, with men grabbing others by the "neckcloth" and collar, and one man (Hilton) going after another with an oar. Such violence was exacerbated by the prevalence of rum and wine, of which the Shoalers drank in abundance. John Josselyn, in *Two Voyages to New England*, wrote that after a successful fishing trip the fishermen of Hog Island would spend days at their cups, unwilling (and unable) to pursue their vocation. The few more moderate fishermen drank, according to Dudley Tyng, "a liquor which they called *bounce*, composed of two thirds *spruce beer* and one third *wine*."

Such men and women clearly required moral and religious mentorship. The first ministers to serve the fishermen of the Isles of Shoals were established at Strawbery Banke, York, and Richmond's Island (off the Maine coast). Such was Joseph Hull, an Anglican priest educated at Oxford. Hull had served for years as a rector in England before voyaging to Massachusetts in 1635. Hull was a founder of the towns of Weymouth and Barnstable before he moved north to Gorges's colony, performing ministerial duties at York as well as Hog Island and Smuttynose. Hull served

Fishing for cod from a dory. *Drawing by H.W. Elliott and Captain J.W. Collins. Courtesy of the National Oceanic and Atmospheric Administration.*

the islanders from 1643 to 1652, during years when in England civil war was brought about by religious conflict between Anglicans and Puritans. Perhaps because the Puritans defeated the Anglicans and established the Commonwealth, the Puritans of Massachusetts felt empowered to impose their will upon the Anglicans of the Piscataqua Valley, Maine, and Isles of Shoals. The Anglican Hull was forced out, replaced by the Puritan minister John Brock. Educated at Harvard College, Brock served the parish at Rowley, Massachusetts, until he relocated to Hog Island, where he served for ten years. Hagiographers such as the Reverend Cotton Mather lauded Brock as follows:

> *He was a pious youth, a good man, a laborious minister, preaching not only on the Sabbath, but frequent lectures to the members of the church, and to young people. These extraordinary religious exercises, he considered as means of rendering his public labours effectual to the people of his charge. He was faithful and diligent in his pastoral visits; and from his happy talent in conversation, he made them instructive and useful. So remarkable was he for his piety and holiness, that it was said of him, by an eminent and venerable divine, "he dwelt as near heaven as any man upon earth." Like the martyr Stephen, he was a man full of faith and of the Holy Ghost.*

Such was his saintliness, according to Mather, that Reverend Brock performed miracles and had the gift of prophecy. One fine day for fishing, for example, his parishioners came to him to request that, rather than engage in worship on this predetermined day as they had agreed, they be excused to pursue their vocation. Brock told them it was not the Lord's will that they ignore their religious duties, and advised against the plan. Five men followed his direction, but thirty did not. Brock preached to the recalcitrant thirty, as they prepared to depart: "As for you, who are determined to neglect your duty to God, and go a fishing, I say unto you, catch fish if you can. But as for you, who will tarry and worship the Lord Jesus Christ, I will pray unto him for you, that you may catch fish till you are weary." The prophecy came true, of course: the thirty caught five fish, while the five, the next day, caught five hundred. Who knows what Brock could have done with five fish and a few loaves of bread! On another occasion, a faithful parishioner lamenting the loss of his boat, having broken its moorings in a squall, Brock piously replied, "Go home, honest man, I will mention the matter to the Lord; you will have your boat against [sic] tomorrow." Miraculously, the next day "the poor man came to him rejoicing that his boat was found; the anchor of another vessel, that was undesignedly cast upon it, having strangely brought it up, from the unknown bottom, where it had been sunk."

Upon the Restoration of King Charles II to the throne in England, and the emergence again of Anglican authority, Brock resigned his position at Hog Island in 1662 and took the parish in Reading, Massachusetts. Joseph Hull, having spent the intervening ten years in England, returned to America in 1662, briefly serving the parish at Oyster River (Durham) in the Piscataqua Valley, before returning once again to Hog Island, where he served until his death in 1665.

The economy of Hog Island and Smuttynose continued to thrive during these years. One contemporary in 1660 wrote that "the Isles of Shooles [is] one of the best places for ffishing [sic] in the land." During these years the inhabitants sought to form themselves into a lawful township, and petitioned the General Court at Boston for this purpose. The petition gave as reasons for the request the distance involved in the Shoalers having to attend court at York (Maine), which the waves and weather often disrupted, and the uncomfortable sense of dependence upon the town militias of the mainland, when the Isles had upwards of one hundred able men who were willing to form a militia. The General Court denied several such petitions for incorporation as a township, though did allow a local court to be established to determine minor civil cases. Not until after the Restoration, in 1661, was the town of Appledore incorporated on Hog Island. The inhabitants of the Isles of Shoals continued under the government of Massachusetts until 1679, when Charles II decreed that New Hampshire be created as a separate province from Massachusetts. Former Shoaler John Cutt became president of the new province. The status

Fishermen in dory hauling in a catch. *From photograph by T.W. Smillie. Courtesy of the National Oceanic and Atmospheric Administration.*

of the Isles of Shoals remained uncertain, however, for several years, when the islands were divided between the District of Maine (part of Massachusetts) and New Hampshire. The northern islands of Duck, Hog (Appledore), Smuttynose, Malaga and Cedar were henceforth connected to Maine, while the southern islands of Star, Lunging (Londoner's) and White came under the jurisdiction of New Hampshire.

Toward the end of the seventeenth century, whether for religious or political reasons, the inhabitants tended to congregate on Star Island, and the township of Appledore on Hog Island was eventually abandoned. By this time of the 1680s, the meetinghouse on Appledore was decaying, such that in 1685 the County Court at York had charged the inhabitants of Appledore "for their neglect in not maintaining a sufficient meeting house for the worship of God." One reason for the exodus was that the Shoalers preferred the jurisdiction (and lower taxes) of New Hampshire over Massachusetts. Antiquarian John Jenness recorded another possible reason for the move; Star Island was easier to defend, perhaps because of all the Isles, it alone is surrounded by almost uninterrupted islands, ledges and shoals, providing a natural defense. During these years, from 1689 to 1763, New France and the British American colonies were frequently at war: King William's War (1689–1697), Queen Anne's War (1703–1713), Dummer's War (1722–1725), King George's War (1744–1749) and the French-Indian

New Hampshire coasline, with the Isles seen in the background. *Courtesy of Benjamin Lawson.*

War (1754–1763). The British Americans were often on the defense, as the French were adept at persuading their Native American allies that English power must be destroyed to preserve the Eastern forests that had for so long been inhabited by Algonquin tribes. During King William's War in 1696, Abenaki raiders from Maine attacked settlements at the Piscataqua Valley before being pursued to the coast at Rye, where the Abenakis took to their birch canoes and headed out to sea, rounding the Isles of Shoals on the eastern side then heading up the Maine coast. During King William's and Queen Anne's War, the French repeatedly contemplated wiping out English settlements on the Maine and New Hampshire coast, including the Isles of Shoals. Projected attacks, however, never took place until Dummer's War, when the Native Americans, having captured a score of English fishing boats, attacked the Isles, stole a few shallops, and retreated to the Penobscot Valley, the colonial militia in pursuit. British Americans anticipated a French-Indian attack on the Shoals during King George's War and a small fortification was constructed on Star Island, armed with nine small cannon. The New Hampshire provincial government granted Gosport "fifteen pounds to purchase ammunition, the money to be paid to ye selectmen of said Gosport for ye use of said town out of ye publick Treasure." The Shoalers never had to resort to using the cannon to defend themselves from the French, and the fort was dismantled at the beginning of the Revolutionary War to keep it out of British hands.

Chapter 2

God's Port

The scant records of the lives of the inhabitants of the Isles of Shoals during the seventeenth century speak of the coarse, rude simplicity of the people, who come across as swearing, hard-drinking, violent sons and daughters of Adam and Eve, who knew how to sin and did their very best to illustrate this peculiar talent in diverse ways. At the same time, rather like children, they were quick to repent and seek the forgiveness of their fellow Shoalers and of God. There was a stark innocence in these people, innocence bred of ignorance and lack of education as well as a rudimentary, sincere piety, a profound sense of awe toward and complete awareness of dependence upon God. The contradictory character of the Shoalers, these pious sinners, originated from the singular experience of life on the Isles of Shoals. Summers on the Isles are mild enough, the pleasant temperatures and cool winds driving away July and August heat creating an environment that has made the Isles of Shoals a destination for tourists and a sanctuary for the embattled soul. Winters on the Shoals, however, are only for the hardiest man and woman, he and she who can withstand the cold, wet easterlies that bring pounding waves and gale-force winds that rake the rocky islands unimpeded by wind breaks of any sort. The pleasant, cool fogs of summer give way in winter to icy fogs that moisten and freeze rocks, boats, oars, clothes and people. Such moist cold is driven away with a raging fire and hot rum on a full stomach. But the warmth and smells of the hearth require work. For the Shoalers their winter work involved terrible hardship, the men braving the cold waves and wind, spending long days bringing in the catch with hands wet and raw with cold. The open fishing shallops provided no protection from the elements, and fishermen would spend their days wetted to the skin, cold to the bone, longing for the end of day and the return home to warmth and security. As they rowed their shallops toward the islands, bringing their flagging strength to bear on the oars, fighting the contrary winds and waves, the rocky isles were an oasis amid extremes of privation and suffering, a port to bring the day's fears and weariness to an end, a cold and rock-strewn salvation from the violent sea. No wonder that the fishermen referred to the port on Star Island as God's Port.

Assisting the returning mariners were the ministers of God's Port. Reverend Samuel Belcher, of Ipswich, Massachusetts, a Harvard graduate, succeeded Joseph Hull in 1665 and lived on Smuttynose. Reverend Belcher motivated the Shoalers in 1671 to make a "free Contribution" every Sabbath for "the supply of their necessitys of poor, sicke, aged, and [diseased] or decreped persons." Toward the end of his time with the Shoalers, the inhabitants of Star Island built a new meetinghouse on the highest part of the island. The church spire, John Jenness noted in *Isles of Shoals*, was a seamark for ships; at night a light in the church belfry served as an early lighthouse. Even so, the Shoalers did not support well the ministry of Belcher's successor, Reverend Daniel Greenleafe, who served the islanders for about twenty years. In 1705 Massachusetts paid Greenleafe fourteen pounds, and New Hampshire chipped in six pounds, to supplement the meager salary provided by the fishers of Star Island. Greenleafe left soon after. In the interim, Theophilus Cotton, a Harvard graduate in 1701, preached briefly at the Shoals until he took charge of the parish at Hampton Falls. The Reverend Joshua Moody, a native of Salisbury, Massachusetts, and minister at Ipswich, Massachusetts, supplied the parish from 1706 to 1732. When Moody was unavailable, Reverend Cotton filled in; the Shoalers became so used to him that for many years they brought their children to Hampton Falls to be baptized, even though the Falls River, on which Hampton Falls was built, was a good deal farther than Hampton, Rye, Newcastle, or Portsmouth. Even so the church records of Gosport indicate that Gosport children were baptized by ministers up and down the seacoast, which indicates how intermittent Reverend Moody's service was. The records of the church at Hampton Falls notes the difficulty of Reverend Cotton's service to the Shoalers; the voyage was a good twenty miles from Hampton Falls to Gosport, and Cotton was obese and in ill health. Indeed, he died in 1726 after a brief time of service on the Isles. (Reverend Cotton in his will left a legacy for the as-yet-unformed parish at Gosport.) According to Dudley Tyng, author of *Description of Isles of Shoals*, published in 1800, Reverend Moody on one occasion preached to his congregation in the wake of the loss of a fishing boat and crew. Seeking to emphasize the dependence of fishermen upon God's will, Moody preached, "Supposing, my brethren, any of you should be taken short in the bay, in a N. E. storm, your hearts trembling with fear, and nothing but death before

Schooner at anchor awaiting the end of a winter gale. *Drawing by H.W. Elliott and Captain J.W. Collins. Courtesy of the National Oceanic and Atmospheric Administration.*

you, whither would your thoughts turn? What would you do?" One fisher with more wit than piety responded, "Why I should immediately hoist the foresail and scud away for Squam," a harbor on Cape Ann.

The General Court of New Hampshire incorporated the town of Gosport on Star Island in December 1715. Although early records of Gosport are scant, one surviving document from the provincial records is revealing of the Gosport inhabitants' view of their town. In April 1721, the townspeople petitioned the General Court for relief from their tax burden. Selectman Richard Yeton, speaking for the islanders, adopted a conciliatory tone toward the General Court, attributing their lack of tax contributions to their unfortunate circumstances.

> *The people are very few in number & most of them are men of no Substance, live only by their daily fishing and near one third of them are single men and threaten to remove and leave us, if the tax be laid which will prove our utter ruine if our fishermen leave us. The charge and expence which they are at in the support of the ministry is as great as the people can bear at present it having cost them but lately the sum of Two Hundred pounds for that end in building a Meeting house—which is not yet all paid. The Government have here tofore* [sic] *encouraged them that they should be exempted from paying Province Taxes while they Exprest their forwardness in so good a Service.*

New Hampshire coast from Rye to Hampton. *Courtesy of Benjamin Lawson.*

Besides, Selectman Yeton explained, the inhabitants "live on a Rock in the Sea do have not any priviledge of right in common Lands, as other Inhabitants in the respective Towns have."

Landless, relying only on the harvest of the sea, the fishermen of Gosport daily plowed through the crest and valleys of the Gulf of Maine seeking the rich harvest of fish such as haddock, pollock, herring and flounder. Such fish were, however, insignificant next to cod, which did not require salting and packing in a barrel, and could be dried in the sun. Ever since the early 1500s, the greatest fisheries were off the coast of Newfoundland at the Grand Banks, at the St. Pierre Bank at the Gulf of St. Lawrence, and Banquereau Bank and Sable Bank off of Nova Scotia. Here cod of various sizes, including some of over one hundred pounds, were taken in great numbers by Basque, French, Portuguese and English fishermen. By the time the Isles of Shoals were settled, and in the eighteenth century when Gosport was incorporated, the cod fishery was still thriving at Browns Bank south of Nova Scotia and east of Monhegan Island, and at the Gorges Bank east-southeast of the Isles of Shoals. Dudley Tyng wrote that shortly after the incorporation of Gosport the cod fishery "increased to that degree, that three or four ships used to load here, annually, with winter and spring merchantable fish, for Bilboa, in Spain, and smaller vessels for other places."

"Description of four remarkable Fishes, taken near the Piscataqua in New Hampshire" by William Peck. 1804. In *Memoirs of the American Academy of Arts and Sciences. Courtesy of the National Oceanic and Atmospheric Administration.*

Much fish was shipped the short distance to Portsmouth, where Piscataqua merchant ships carried the cargo to the West Indies.

The demand for cod throughout the Atlantic world was due to its ease at preservation and superior eating when cooked. The best season for catching cod was late winter and early spring; such winter fish, called *dumb* fish, were "fairer, larger, and thicker fish" than those caught in summer. During the 1600s and 1700s, cod were incredibly abundant in the Gulf of Maine. Fishermen used hand lines with baited hooks; the challenge was not what is typical in fishing—patience—but rather having the energy to bring up large fish from the cold water recurrently, as the hook would scarcely hit the water before a fish pounced on the bait. Fishermen used lines rather than nets, working in teams of half a dozen men per shallop, a small, open boat, broad more than long, pointed at both ends, and propelled by oars or sail. Fishers fished during the morning hours in winter and often at night in summer. According to Jeremy Belknap, who lived at the Piscataqua Valley and knew the fisheries of seacoast towns and Gosport, "the cod fishery is carried on either by boats or schooners," which make three trips to the Banks in a season." In Belknap's time of the late 1700s, fishermen used whaleboats, rather like shallops. These were "light and swift…rowed either with two or four oars." Another oar served as the rudder. These boats were curved to a

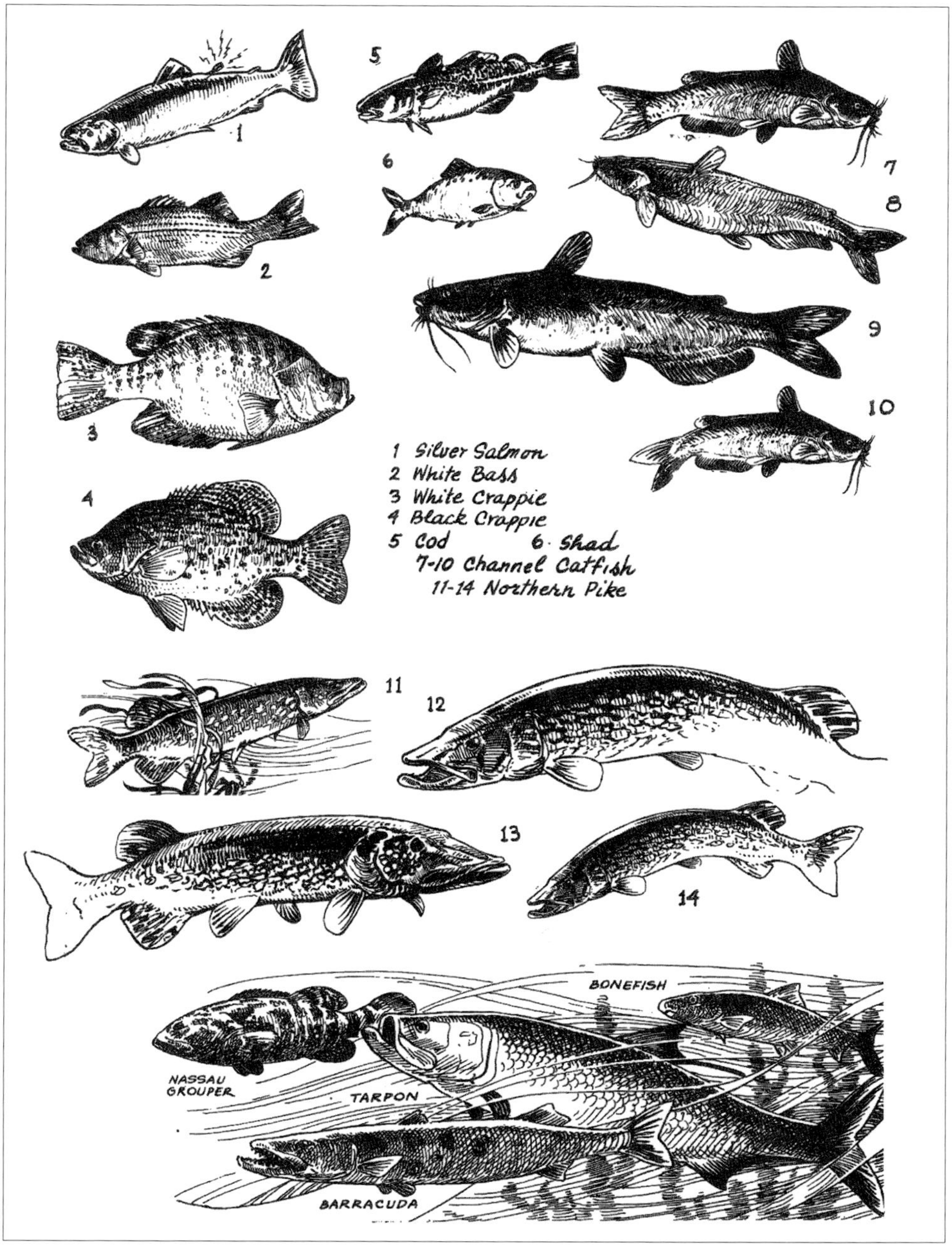

Fresh and salt water fish of the waters of northern New England. *Courtesy of the U.S. Fish and Wildlife Service Digital Library System.*

point in both bow and stern, which allowed them to "move with the utmost celerity on the surface of the ocean. Schooners are generally from twenty to fifty tuns, and carry six or seven men, and one or two boys. When they make a tolerable fare, they bring home five or six hundred quintals of fish." Schooners were typically rigged fore and aft, that is, the sails were parallel, rather than perpendicular, to the length of the boat. "The fish of the summer and fall fares is divided into two sorts, the one called merchantable, and the other Jamaica fish. These sorts are white, thick and less firm. The Jamaica fish is the smallest, thinnest and most broken. The former is exported to Europe, the latter to the West India Islands." The Gosport fishermen, once they filled the boat, which might take only half a day, returned to port, where others, a shore crew of fishers and fishwives, prepared the catch. Shoalers engaged in dry rather than wet fishing; the latter required packing the fish in salt on board the boat immediately after the catch was gutted. Dry fishing, however, involved an extensive operation on land. "The fish," according to Dudley Tyng, "in the first place, are thrown from the boats in piles on the shore." The fishers piled the fish typically onto wooden stages, a wharf extending from the shore. "The *cutter* then takes them and cuts their throats, and rips open their bellies. In this state he hands them to the *header*, who takes out the entrails, (detaching the livers, which are preserved for the sake of the oil they contain) and breaks off their heads. The *splitter* then takes out the back-bone, and splits them completely open, and hands them to the *salter*, who salts and piles them in bulk, where they lie from ten to twenty hours, as is most convenient. The shoremen and the women then wash and spread them on the flakes," which were wooden platforms of driftwood erected several feet off the ground "Here they remain three or four weeks, according to the weather; during which time they are often turned, piled in faggots and then spread again, till they are completely cured for the market." Once prepared, cured fish were stored in sheds, called tilts, connected to the stages. "The dumb fish is consumed chiefly in New-England, and is considered by connoisseurs in fish, the best in the world." Belknap recorded another way of making dumb fish. This "large thick fish," after "being properly salted and dried, is kept alternately above and under ground, till it becomes so mellow as to be denominated dumb fish. This fish, when boiled, is red, and is eaten generally on Saturdays." The cod had other uses besides food. "Its liver is preserved in casks," Belknap wrote, "and boiled down to oyl, which is used by curriers of leather. The tongues and sounds are pickled in small kegs, and make a luxurious, viscid food. The heads are fat and juicy; but most of those which are caught at sea are thrown away. Of those which are caught near home, the greater part become the food of swine." The historian Belknap noted that the golden age of the New Hampshire fishery was around the time Gosport was incorporated, when "seven or eight ships were loaded" with dumb fish "annually for Spain and Portugal."

A pink voyaging to herring fishing grounds. *From a photograph by T.W. Smillie. Courtesy of the National Oceanic and Atmospheric Administration.*

Living on these small islands of little more than six hundred acres were, according to Richard Henry Dana writing in 1843, over a thousand people. "I could hardly credit the story that these islands had supported so many persons," Dana wrote, "and should not but upon the best authority. They must have imported all their wood and nearly all their hay and vegetables"—although the sea provided driftwood to meet some of their needs. Dana also found it hard to believe the "tradition that a school flourished on Hog Island at which the sons of men of fortune in Boston and other parts of the main land were fitted for college."

The Shoalers of the early eighteenth century worked at common tasks of a joint occupation, pursuing the singular goal of gaining their sustenance from the sea, residing in a close-knit community. Personal and public lives merged; few individual secrets could be hidden from the whole. Living on the verge of society and the endless ocean, there was a subtle sense of equality, even if eighteenth-century life often held views to the contrary. General similarity of wealth and income was such that town leaders, their wives and families, put on few airs, and dress was the same for the biggest as well as the smallest man. There were a few slaves on the Isles, serving as personal servants or nurses, but there were a few free blacks as well. In 1733, for example, according to the town records, "Black Charles" earned two pounds "for Ring'g ye Bell & Tak'g care of the Meeting house." Charles was, in other words, a sexton. Few inhabitants had special rights, and whenever a townsperson tried to assume a privilege, there was quick recourse to the selectmen, constable and county courts. An exception was seating in the meetinghouse, which was done in an orderly fashion, as elsewhere in New England congregational churches, according to males and females, young and old, rich and poor. Government involved only the males, who sat in assembly (with one of their number serving as moderator) to elect annually the town officers, such as those who ran daily town affairs, the selectmen, three in number. The town treasurer received taxes and dispersed payments, for example to the poor. The constable collected taxes and fines for disorder (such as allowing hogs to run about goodwives' gardens) and kept the peace. There was sometimes a schoolmaster, whenever a pastor was unavailable to keep school. Two or three men served yearly as "Tything Men," collecting the parish rates and dispersing funds for the church. Two men served as "Cullers of Fish," examining the daily catch and separating the good and useful from the bad and waste fish. The "Corders of Wood," often two in number, kept track of wood imports and dispersed them for fuel and other purposes to the inhabitants. The town clerk (or "clark," as it was frequently pronounced and written) recorded the minutes of the town meetings in an often illegible and unintelligible hand. Besides their daily task of fishing, the Gosport inhabitants worked together for special needs, such as repairs of the meetinghouse and preparations for defense.

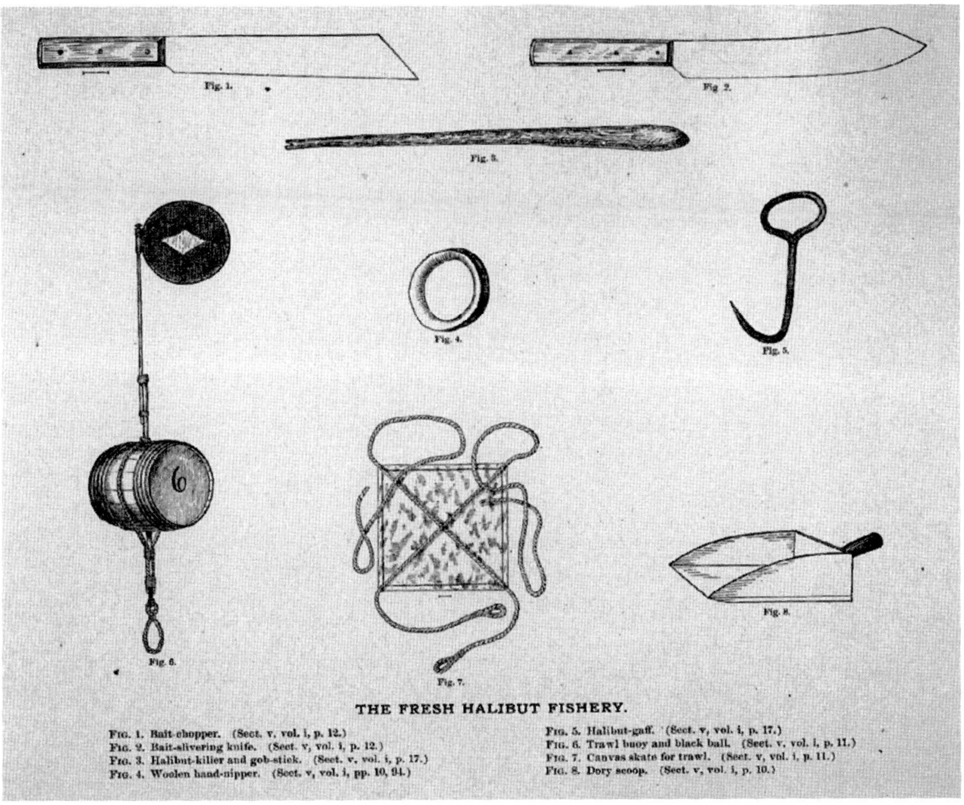

Tools for fishing and preparing fish for market. *Drawing by Captain J.W. Collins. Courtesy of the National Oceanic and Atmospheric Administration.*

The core of existence, the *raison d'etre* of the inhabitants of Gosport, was the cod fishery. Fish was their food, the topic of conversation, the basis for memory, the hope for the future. Goods for home-life, supplies for fishing, were purchased with fish. The smell of fish invaded the homes, boats, clothing, perspiration, breath and air of Gosport. The aroma of boiled fish; the cold, stark odor of fresh fish; the rank smells of rotting fish prevailed over the Isles and their people. Fish was their money, the means of exchange. Debts and salaries were paid in fish. The Reverend John Tucke, for example, who was minister at Gosport from 1732 to 1773, received his annual salary in "merchantable winter fish, a quintal a man," which by the mid-eighteenth century equaled about one hundred pounds.

John Tucke was brought to the Isles of Shoals through the agency of several seacoast ministers, particularly Nathaniel Morrill, the minister of the parish at Rye, a town parallel to Gosport on the New Hampshire coast. Reverend Morrill encouraged the townspeople to organize a parish at Gosport, and to employ a permanent minister. Reverend Morrill recorded the proceedings in a 1729 document inserted into the Gosport church records:

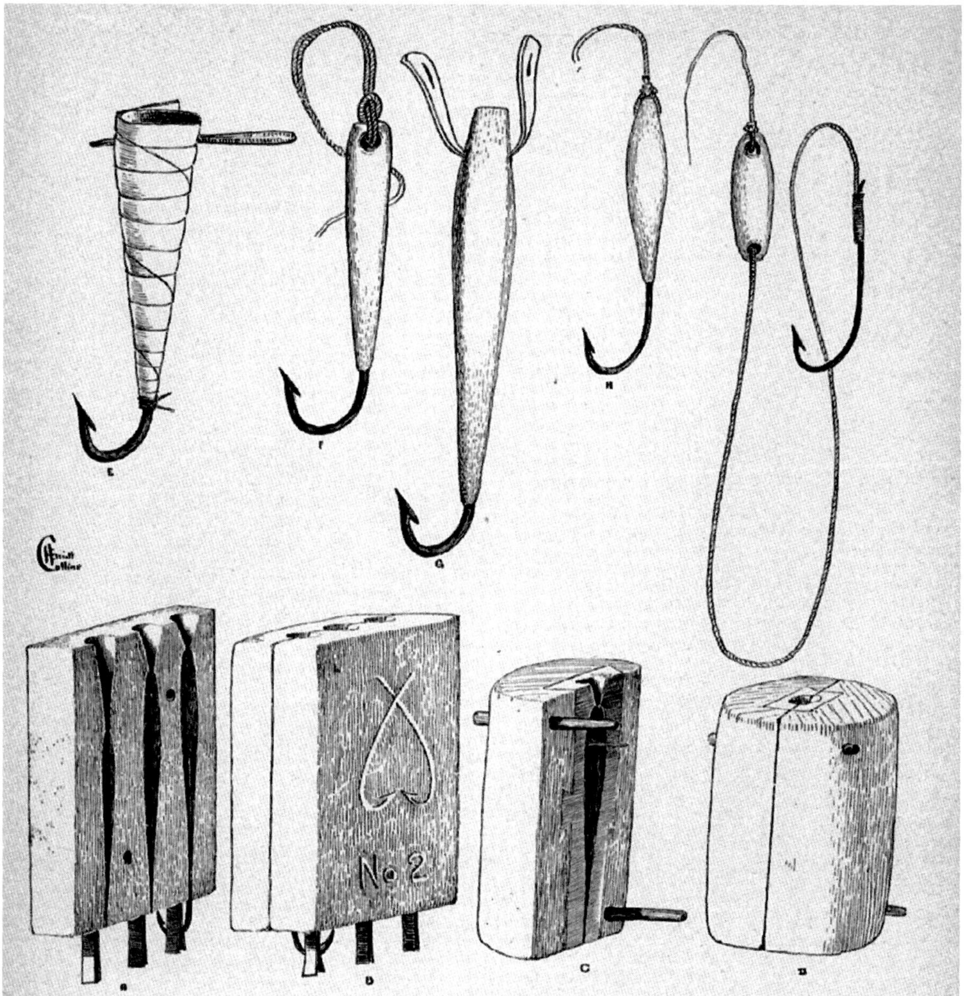

THE MACKEREL HOOK FISHERY.

Jigs and jig-molds: A, one side of soapstone jig-mold, showing method of setting hook; B, soapstone jig-mold, closed; C, one side of lead jig-mold made by fishermen; D, lead jig-mold, closed; E, old-style paper jig-mold; F and G, types of jigs, natural size, cast in paper molds; H, type of jig, of medium size, cast in soapstone molds. I, mackerel bobber. (Sect. v, vol. i, p. 278.)

Drawings by H. W. Elliott and Capt. J. W. Collins.

Fishing hooks for catching mackerel. *Courtesy of the National Oceanic and Atmospheric Administration.*

> *Anno Domini 1729. Sometime in the Spring of this year, at an Association of Ministers at Hampton, the Case of the People of the Isle of Shoales with respect to their being without an Ordain'd Minister was consider'd, & it was tho't expedient to send over a Minister or Two to see how the People Stood affected towards the Settlement of a Minister among them, & accordingly some Ministers were chosen to go over, but they not going, this Affair for the Present came to nothing. After this the People themselves sent over to an Association at Portsmouth desiring their Advice & Direction & they chose ye Rev'd Mr Morril*

> *of Rye to go over & see if he could gather a Church among them. Accordingly Mr Morril came over & the People readily agreed to have a Church Gather'd amongst them & that the 29th of June 1729 be observed as a Day of Fasting & Prayer. And accordingly ye 29th of June 1729 was kept &* [the parishioners that] *Morning met at Mr Joshua Moodys Lodging &* [there adopted the Statement of Confession and Statement of] *Covenant & then they went to Meeting where was made known what was done in Private & those Persons did in Publick Enter into Covenant with God & with one another.*

Reverend Morrill then addressed the new parishioners of Gosport, praying that "may God Give you a Pastor after His own Heart, may He Thrust forth a Labourer into this part of His Vineyard, which God of His Infinite Mercy Grant it may be Speedily! Amen." It took three years for Morrill's prayer to be answered in the person of the Reverend John Tucke.

John Tucke, born in 1702 in Hampton, grew up among the marshy landscape and the long sandy beaches of Hampton, where he could look out upon the Atlantic and see the Isles of Shoals floating on the surface. Hampton lacked a good harbor, but had extensive tidal marshes, flat and green, beautiful to behold, notwithstanding the repugnant odor. Tucke was the son of the Hampton town clerk who served as a representative to the New Hampshire General Court; the elder John Tucke was also a church deacon. The younger John Tucke matriculated at Harvard, where he graduated in 1723 intent on a career in the ministry; like many Harvard graduates he served under a local minister while he studied for his master's degree. In 1724 Tucke married Mary Dole, daughter of Hampton physician Benjamin Dole; the two set up housekeeping at Hampton, while Tucke served as an itinerant minister for various New Hampshire parishes, such as at Chester and Hampton Falls. Meanwhile, while living at Hampton, the couple had three children—born in 1726, 1729 and 1731—but all died in infancy. In 1729, when the parish at Chester offered him a position with a good salary, Tucke refused, citing "Weighty Reasons," namely the death of two children two months apart. His firstborn son, John, died three months shy of his third birthday on April 29, a little over two months after the death of their newborn infant daughter on February 23. At Hampton, John Tucke felt God's presence, in some moments feeling as blessed as Abraham in his marriage, wealth and gift of children; at other times he felt as did Job, suffering according to God's inscrutable will.

Tucke continued as an itinerant for two years, including preaching at Gosport, when the fishers and their wives decided that they wanted Reverend Tucke to be their permanent minister. Significantly, the surviving Gosport town records begin on December 11, 1732, with the selectmen Captain Robert Downes, Francis Combs and George Collings calling the inhabitants to meet at Captain Downes's home to decide whether or not to call John

Rye Harbor at low tide. *Courtesy of Benjamin Lawson.*

Tucke to the ministry. Participation in town meetings in early America was restricted to adult male citizens. Those of Gosport met December 13 and town clerk William Sanderson recorded the proceedings:

> *The Question being ask'd at the said meeting by the moderator whether it was their minds to make choice of the Reverend Mr John Tooke to be their Minister and whether they did chuse him to settle among them in the work of the Ministry in case he should accept...and it pass'd in the affermative...It was al'so Voted, to give & allow the Reverend Mr John Tooke annually for his Support & maintenance one hundred and ten Pounds mony or bills of Credit, so long as it shall please God to continue him among us in the work of the Ministry... It was al'so Voted that the Reverend Mr John Tooke should have two thirds of his annual Salary allow'd and pay'd him annually by the Last of May and the other third by the last of September...It was al'so voted to give the Reverend Mr John Tooke fifty pounds in Mony by the Last of May next towards building him a House, in Case he chuseth to Build a House himself but in case he should hereafter remove from us he shall be oblidg'd to give us the refusal of buying the House and abate us fifty pounds in the price. It was al'so voted to give to the Reverend Mr John Tooke a convenient place to sett his House upon & a garden Spot...It was al'so voted that Mr Andrew Mace Mr Samuel Sanders & Mr Thomas Lambert be a committee to Treat with the Rev'd Mr John Tooke to acquaint him what is done at this meeting...It was al'so voted that they would proceed to ordain the Rev'd Mr John Tooke some Convenient time next Spring in case he accepts of what is above voted.*

Fishing schooner seeking a fresh catch of mackerel. *From photograph by T.W. Smillie. Courtesy of the National Oceanic and Atmospheric Administration.*

The generous terms of the offer indicated the seriousness of the inhabitants in wanting a minister to settle among them. The committee of three Gosport fishers duly approached John Tucke with the offer. Tucke was long in responding, however, because in the intervening period, John and Mary Tucke experienced "a very heavy Stroake of Providence"—their son Benjamin, eleven months old, died in March. The townspeople were unwilling to give up, and met again at the end of April to reaffirm their call to Tucke according to the same terms as before, with the exception of an additional inducement that he was granted the privilege to have a cow on Gosport. Tucke responded April 28 that "hopeing that there is a prospect of doing Good among you, I rely'ing on the Strength of Divine Grace accept of Your call to me." Tucke added, by way of friendly pastoral warning, that the "Lord ordain'd that they which preach the Gospel should live of the Gospel. The same I Expect amongst you."

Notwithstanding that New England Puritans were not given to ceremony, the event of an ordination was too important to take lightly. Surrounding ministers would join together to preach, charge the minister with his duty and present the right hand of fellowship. The date of the ordination was set for July 1732; the selectmen sent letters to ministers Nathaniel Morrill of Rye, Jabez Fitch of Portmouth, John Newmarch of Kittery, and Nathaniel Gookin. They duly arrived and on July 26, Reverend Newmarch gave the charge, Reverend Morrill gave the right hand of fellowship and Reverend Fitch preached the sermon, "Gospel Ministers Considered under the Similitude of Fishers of Men."

Tucke's ordination at Gosport and subsequent forty years of service to the fishers and fishwives was a perfect match for him and for them. Tucke was a fisher, perhaps not in his profession, not actively, but implicitly, for to live on the Isles was to be intricately part of the fishing community. The sights and sounds and the daily living and conversation of the community were of fishing. He constantly dealt with fishing and fishermen. Daily he thought of it. Fishing was life, self-contained on this island. So Tucke was a fisherman in all aspects of his life—emotional, mental, spiritual, economic, political, social—though not in his daily earning of a living. The islanders fished from the sea, daily bringing forth their catch from the deep, redeeming themselves from privation and hunger. John Tucke fished from the sea of men, bringing forth his catch from the depths of loneliness, despair and suffering, redeeming himself and others from the privation of sin, the hunger for the divine. John Tucke empathized with the men and women of the Isles of Shoals. He not only led them, he personified them, in a sense became them, which is precisely how one becomes a fisher of men.

Chapter 3

Fisher of Men

John Tucke's new life at Gosport demanded patience to withstand the misbehavior, the sin, of a riotous people; charity to forgive their many transgressions of the laws of man and God; perseverance to never give up the fight for the ways of righteousness; courage to look danger in the face but never to give in to it; faith to withstand constant suffering but never to bow down to it; love to embrace others, sinners as well as saints, as brothers and sisters, as fellow children of God. The Shoalers looked to Tucke as lost sheep to a shepherd. Tucke led his people by word and by example in the endless struggle against sin, for he too lived his life on a rock in the sea, struggling against the elements, the cold, the loneliness, the danger, the endless story of death, disaster and sorrow, the isolation of the soul. The Shoalers experienced seemingly unremitting strokes from Providence. Tucke, who knew these strokes as well, refused to lose faith, and used suffering and error as a means to find solace in God. Tucke, the spiritual leader of these people, made the words of the sermon and scripture become flesh, hence showing the power of belief in a way words alone cannot accomplish.

The day after his ordination, Tucke took action. Representatives of the church met at the "Minister's House," which indicates either that the town was using a house for a parsonage or that Tucke had been at the Isles sufficiently long that he had already set up housekeeping. The first request that the parishioners had of their pastor was that he administer "ye Sacrament of ye Lord's Supper…by reason some of ye Brethrens long absence from home [they] going to Sea ye next Week." Henceforth, the parishioners agreed that the Lord's Supper be administered once per month.

Two Shoalers, William Muchamore and Andrew Mace, were made deacons of the parish. Reverend Tucke was very much a child of the Protestant Reformation, fully embracing—as did other New England Puritans—the spirit of reform in worship, eschewing the seven sacraments of Catholicism and Anglicanism for the two sacraments of Lord's Supper and baptism. Persons wanting to enter into full communion with the church had to first confide to Reverend Tucke "the sense of the hope that is in them," followed by a full exposition of their feelings of faith to the entire congregation. Tucke believed that holidays with an apparent pagan origin, such as Christmas and Easter, be eschewed. The church service itself was simple, without pretense either in the minister's vestments and demeanor or in the liturgy and exterior and interior appearance of the church building. The sole source of Christian theology and practice was the reading of the word in the Old and New Testaments.

Tucke instituted the practice of confession of sin to the entire parish at meeting rather than to a priest in isolation. In March 1733, for example, the church declared that parishioner Samuel Emery "had lately been Guilty of Drinking to Excess," to which behavior he must confess before being allowed to take communion. Several weeks later Emery confessed and asked for forgiveness, which was granted by Reverend Tucke and because of which Emery once again enjoyed full communion within the parish. The shepherd believed that the entire flock should be on guard against sin among each member. Leaders of the parish were to speak to such people who were not living according to the "Rule of the Gospel," to try to "Preserve Peace & Brotherly Love, to Prevent Strife & to Heal Division among us, & in a word to take Care to Maintain the Honour of God and ye Credit of Religion among us." Parishioner Andrew Mace felt the united displeasure of the parish in January 1740 because of his "Excessive Drinking & taking God's Name in Vain;" in addition he was "contemptuous" when Reverend Tucke tried to talk to him about his sins, and complained of "lies" being spread about him and the "foes" among the parishioners out to get him "only because he was poor." Mace was excommunicated, as it were, from the parish for two and a half years, when in June 1742 he appeared before the congregation and made a "Publick Confession that in ye year 1739 he was Twice Guilty of drinking to Excess, & at a particular time Taking ye Name of God in Vain, & that he was guilty of...Sinful Behaviour at ye Church Meeting on Jan'y 4th 17[40] when he was Suspended from this Church, & he was Justly Suspended, & also that he was in ye said Meeting Guilty [of] Uncharitable Reflections which he then uttered, & likewise he had been since guilty of Drinking to Excess at several times. Whereupon ye Church Voted his Restoration to their Communion & Fellowship, & ye Pastour Joyned with ye Church & Pronounced Absolution from All Church Censares & his Restoration to Communion."

In March 1743, Reverend Tucke called upon Samuel Emery again, it having been ten years since he had confessed before the congregation of his propensity to drink. Again the wayward parishioner was seen repeatedly intoxicated, but he denied it to Tucke; the pastor declared that Emery was not allowed to participate at the communion service until he made restitution by confession. "Whereupon," Tucke wrote, "he broke out into a Passion, & uttered many Threatning and Disrespectfull Words, & cast many very Ill Reflections upon me, as he also did ye next Week when I went to him to talk further with him. Since which time he has not only Absented himself from ye Sacrament, but also from the House of God, at least three quarters of his time, as far as I can judge. He has also given himself not only much more than he did before to Drink, but also to Prophane & False Speaking. And it is suppos'd that he is now Run-away, it Being some Weeks since he went from hence, & we have providentially heard of his being not only at Portsmouth, at Newbury, at Malden, but also of his being got as far as to Newport in Rhode Island, from whence we hear he is gone to Sea. Ah, poor Man Whither art thou Runing."

Parishioner Mary Downs on October 4, 1746, "Acknowledged that she had of late in a shameful Passion uttered Rash, Reflecting, Threatning & Profane Words, been Noisy & Contentious." Upon confessing in front of the church congregation, she was forgiven and welcomed back into the fold. Most confessions by women at Gosport involved a breach of the Seventh Commandment against adultery. Of many examples is the following from 1745: "This Day, Margaret Newell made a Publick Confession of Her Breach of ye Seventh Commandment, & Desired that her Child might be Baptized, whereupon ye Church by ye Holding up of their Hands Signified that Her Confession was Satisfactory to them, & that they were Willing that Her Child should be Baptized."

In 1746, Gibbins Mace discovered that when the parish forgave sinners and welcomed them to the sacrament that the fallen could truly be redeemed, as he was voted to be deacon. Mace also became a member of a committee of several parishioners charged with going to inhabitants of the Isles, bringing the recalcitrant back into the fold and seeking to heal discord among people of the islands. By the end of the year, however, Deacon Mace came to doubt his abilities and spirit to serve as deacon, and requested that the parish accept his resignation. The problem, perhaps, was the tremendous degree of "Deadness of Religion, & ye abounding of Sin among us," in Reverend Tucke's words. Indeed, on Christmas Eve 1746, Tucke addressed his church, listing the many sins and errors among them, which included "Unbelief…Profanation of God's Holy Name & Sabbath, ye Great Neglect of God's House & Ordinances, ye Want of Love to God, His Sabbaths, House, Ordinances, Institutions & Commands, ye Want of Brotherly Love, ye Want of a Fellow feeling of ye Burdens & Afflictions of others, ye Great Neglect of Family Worship, & Family government, ye Great Mispence of Time"—in particular Reverend Tucke had in mind the sinful happenings that occurred on Christmas Day. Tucke complained of the "Shameful Drunkenness, Horrid Cursing, Swearing, & Fighting, bitter Exclaiming against such as don't Care, or dare not to Run into ye same Excess of Riot with themselves, firing of Guns, Singing & Dancing, & these things under a Pretence of Religion, to Honor God, & to Give Thanks to Him or sending His Son into ye World, when we no where read in ye Holy Scriptures that God hath Commanded any Particular Day to be Yearly Observed in Commemoration of ye Lord Jesus, His Birth into the World."

Such an outburst against a seemingly innocent holiday such as Christmas occurred during the Great Awakening, a religious controversy that engaged much of colonial America during the 1730s and 1740s. The Great Awakening pitted social conservatives and religious liberals, the Old Lights, against social liberals and religious conservatives, the New Lights. John Tucke was an unusual New Light minister, as he was a man of property, owning land in Hampton and Newbury, as well as a slave owner. Yet he was a revivalist as well, who encouraged and marshaled an outpouring of religious enthusiasm and increasing membership at his Gosport parish. He wrote during the height of the Great Awakening in 1743:

> *I acknowledge the Work in this Land to be a blessed Work of God; And I believe that it is the Duty of Christ's Ministers to give an open conjunct Testimony unto it. I apprehend that there are in one Place and in another certain abominable… Errors, and some Disorders in Practice, which ought to be testify'd against.*

This fisher of men, John Tucke, was also a healer. As a Puritan minister, the most educated person by far on the Isles of Shoals, John Tucke would naturally be best informed about the various concoctions from which medicine is made. The flora of the Isles of Shoals provide the means, in the hands of a competent naturalist and healer, to make herbal medicines to treat the sick and injured. Perhaps Tucke knew that tea made from leaves and the inner bark of the white cedar and the berries of the red cedar treat colds, coughs and arthritis, and poultices of the red cedar can treat skin ailments. Tea made from the petals of the aster, a flowering shrub found on the Isles, treats fevers and intestinal ailments. Colonial physicians used the shrubs sea milkwort and scarlet pimpernel to treat depression and insomnia. St. John's wort is also useful to boost the spirits from a melancholy state. Settlers learned to use bayberry to treat headaches and inflammations. Cod liver oil, so readily available on the islands, was used by the Islanders as a tonic for general health. Tucke was as well a healer of the spirit and soul through his empathy, his ability to see the disease of the mind, which one must heal along with the body. Tucke was able to heal people in a way not completely

Fishermen at anchor for the night. *From sketch by J.S. Ryder. Courtesy of the National Oceanic and Atmospheric Administration.*

physical, in a hidden way of strength, patience, endurance and faith, which has an impact on the flesh, however unseen. When Dudley Tyng visited Gosport in 1799, he learned from the inhabitants that sickness was rare, as the climate was "at all seasons very healthful," and rarely was a physician needed. Tyng deduced from his observations as well as his conversations with the Shoalers, however, that the population was not thriving as they had under Reverend Tucke, who "acted in the double capacity of physician of body and of soul."

Tucke oversaw the most significant events in the lives of the Shoalers—birth, baptism, marriage, communion and burial. Puritan ministers were notable statisticians, and Tucke was exceptional in this regard, keeping track of all parish events. Upon taking charge of the parish at Gosport, Tucke researched the church records of neighboring parishes at Hampton, Rye and Newcastle, recording "the Baptisms…of those belonging to the Isles of Sholes." Tucke's list of baptisms in the church records of Gosport provides a unique record of the people of the Isles of Shoals. Tucke baptized men and women, children and adults, those recently widowed and widowers, children born of proper marriages as well as those born out of wedlock to single mothers or couples recently married. He traveled to other New Hampshire parishes, such as Hampton, North Hampton, Hawke (Danvers) and Rye, for baptisms. Tucke baptized his own children as well as the few slaves of the islands, including his own. In July 1742 Tucke baptized "Peter a Negro child belonging to Samuel Abbot." Two months later he baptized "Candace a Negro Child belonging to Mr. John Tucke." Twenty years later in April 1762 "Dinah, Daut'r of Candace, a Negro, was Baptized." In January 1748 "Dolly a Molatto Child of Sam'l Abbot was Baptized." On August 19, 1733, Tucke baptized his daughter Mary. On August 11, 1734 he baptized his son Samuel. On June 23, 1736 he baptized his daughter Bethiah. These three children as well as two others, Benjamin Dole and Jonathan, besides the first three children born at Hampton to John and Mary Tucke, died in infancy. Out of their eleven children, only three survived to adulthood. For John and Mary, life sparkled and flowed during these years. Death hovered like a fog, enveloping the islands and their lives, coming unexpectedly on a new morning, sometimes harshly, heralding a storm. Other times it came gently and the sun soon rose again. Tucke experienced the joy of marrying his daughter Mary to Mark Walton on April 21, 1766, and his daughter Love to Jeffry Muchamore on June 4, 1766. He baptized his namesake and grandson John Tucke, son of Love and Jeffry Muchamore, on January 29, 1769; his grandson Mark, son of Mary and Mark Walton, on June 3, 1770; and his grandson John Tucke, son of Mary and Mark, on December 13, 1772.

The meticulous records of the church at Gosport reveal John Tucke to have been a historian who penned a narrative of the local struggle of sin and redemption, of conversion, fall and reconciliation. He interpreted the history of himself and his people according to the Puritan historiography (based on the works of Augustine of Hippo) of the city of man seeking the city of God. Gosport symbolized life in miniature, a self-contained civilization with an exclusive history. Gosport was the human story in a nutshell: the struggle, anguish, materialism, primitivism and savagery of humans in the state of nature, the seeking of redemption, cleansing of sin, discovery of the divine. The community of believers, the church, was the means of redemption on these barren Isles. At once an antiquarian, archivist and biographer, Tucke through his record resurrects life, the existence of those long dead, for readers long after, even today. For Tucke, the historical record of Gosport was a pious duty to track human events over time, to reconstruct life in all its forms, good and bad, to recall the memory of past lives and not let them be buried with the dead.

Eighteenth-century New England clergymen saw the fingerprints of God in all natural and human events. It was an irresponsible clergyman indeed who did not engage in scientific inquisition and historical scholarship. John Tucke wore the hat of the scientist, besides that of the historian and physician. As a student of nature, John Tucke was a historian of "Elder Scripture," the image of the Creator in all its forms. As an inquirer, Tucke wanted to know the origins not only of the people on the islands, but of the islands as well, which made him a natural historian of the sea, the islands and their relation to the seacoast. He was interested in the climate of the Isles in respect to comparable places on the mainland. Dudley Tyng was told by an informant at Gosport, "The worthy Mr. Tuck used to say, that, in the winter season, the weather at the Shoals was 'a thin under waistcoat warmer, than in the same parallel of latitude on the main.'" Tucke knew what Celia Thaxter later related in *Among the Isles of Shoals:*

> *The weather becomes of the first importance to the dwellers on the rock; the changes of the sky and sea, the flitting of the coasters to and fro, the visits of the sea-fowl, sunrise and sunset, the changing moon, the northern lights, the constellations that wheel in splendor through the winter night.*

Observing on clear days the distant sandy beaches, indentations of the shoreline, salt marshes, and tall white pines of the seacoast, Tucke thought that the physical outline of the islands fit rather like a puzzle to the outline of the coast of New Hampshire. He therefore "entertained the idea, that these islands, at some former period, joined to some of the points or bluffs, that project from the main, near Hampton." Tyng believed that Reverend Tucke "was eminently learned," particularly in "history and geography…beyond most of his contemporaries."

Later commentators such as Dudley Tyng and Jedidiah Morse, who saw the inhabitants of the Shoals at rock bottom, thought that the time under Tucke was a golden age, when Gosport and surrounding islands flourished. To be sure in comparison to the post-Revolutionary period this account is true, but not everything was rosy under Reverend Tucke. The fishers and fishwives of the Isles never became rich, as they tried to convey to the General Court and Governor of New Hampshire in January 1760:

> *The said Inhabitants have allways chearfully paid their Province Tax with Great Willingness and pleasure, so long as they were of ability and untill the four last years when their Circumstances in life became so low (being only a few poor fishermen) and the necessaries for living being Excessively dearer at the place of their aboad* [abode] *one half more than any other part of the Province… togeather with their other great charge, Supporting the Gospel Ministry among them the fewness of the Inhabitants & their poverty and their few within four years last past being Greatly Reduced they having had thirty Two Ratable poles within that time left them to serve the King or Removed to other places.*

The petition, having stressed the consequences of the French-Indian War upon the Isles in terms of inflation, loss of income and war service of inhabitants, went on to stress that should the tax burden be imposed on Gosport that other young families would remove from there, leaving "none but a few old helpless persons left." Governor Benning Wentworth and his council granted the petition from Gosport, and forgave the tax of "five hundred & Twelve pounds Eight shillings & one penny."

Gulls at the Isles of Shoals. *Courtesy of the U.S. Fish and Wildlife Service Digital Library System.*

In an apparent attempt to improve the economic situation of Gosport, the town petitioned the Governor again in 1766, with the following request:

> *That the situation of the Road & harbour at Gosport Aforesaid is well known to be exposed to the Violence of Winds & seas in many cases & Events which frequently occur by which they often sustain much Loss & Damage which they would gladly Prevent it by any means Feasible:*
> *That it has been Judg'd a Pier or Bason might be so contrived and Built as to be in a Great Measure a security in this Case and a means of great saving to your Petitioners & Preservation of their Property.*
>
> *That to make such a work Effectual a Larger sum woud be demanded than your Petitioners by any means coud raise but as it woud be of very General Utility in its Consequences they flatter themselves the scheme for carrying on such a Building woud meet with suitable Encouragement from many other Persons besides your Petitioners & those who have connections with them.*
>
> *Wherefore your Petitioners Humbly Pray that they may have leave to set up & carry on a Publick Lottery to raise money for the End aforesaid.*

The petition was supported by a huge list of signatures that included influential merchants of Portsmouth. The province responded in the affirmative, though the scheme never came to fruition.

During the subsequent decade leading to the American Revolution, the population of Gosport declined, which was exacerbated by John Tucke's death in 1773. Tucke was worth 160 pounds when he died, though the Shoalers were indebted to him, financially as well as spiritually. He was buried on Gosport in a burial yard called, appropriately, "God's Field." The attempt to replace him had mixed success. A Harvard graduate, the Reverend Jeremiah Shaw of Hampton, preached off and on for several years. The town continued to try to employ a schoolmaster. A small fort, built during King George's War on the western extreme of Star Island, was ordered by the revolutionary government of New Hampshire to be dismantled. The Shoalers continued to trade with the English even after the outbreak of war in April 1775. In September Governor John Wentworth, ousted from Portsmouth a few months earlier, made his last official act from Gosport, proclaiming the New Hampshire assembly adjourned. Knowing that at one point in their history the Shoalers had Anglican, Tory sympathies, the revolutionary government of Massachusetts forced the removal of all inhabitants from Appledore Island in 1775; New Hampshire ordered the same of Star Island and Gosport in January 1776. Most of the Shoalers complied, though some few desperate holdouts stayed throughout the war.

The experiences of those few inhabitants who remained on the Isles of Shoals during the war are lost in time. The cessation of trade and the soaring inflation caused by the war stressed New Englanders up and

Harbor at Newburyport. *Courtesy of Russell M. Lawson.*

down the coast. Coastal communities often experienced the brunt of the war's violence—Falmouth, Maine, was largely destroyed by a British naval bombardment in 1775. The narrow, winding and well-defended Piscataqua preserved Portsmouth from direct attack. But the economy of the town declined precipitously. One of the biggest burdens was the growing number of poor, as inflation destroyed the lifestyles of those on set incomes, and as jobs related to fishing and trade declined in the face of British control of coastal waters. Inhabitants of the Isles of Shoals, complying with the demands of Massachusetts and New Hampshire that they leave the islands, fled to familiar towns where they hoped to be welcomed and assisted. Many went to Newburyport at the mouth of the Merrimack River; most went to Portsmouth. The inhabitants of Portsmouth had for many years concerned themselves with the affairs of the Isles of Shoals. When the war began, the town provided assistance to their neighbors at Gosport, but soon petitioned the New Hampshire revolutionary legislature that the "Poor on the Isles of Shoals be relieved out of the Public Treasury, to ease the Burthens of this Town which has been at great Expense on their Account, & at a time when we are unable to Maintain our own." Parenthetically, the petition reveals that in 1776 there were enough inhabitants at the Isles to cause a burden in providing them with economic relief. In the 1779 "Statement of the Condition of Matters in Town," the citizens of Portsmouth complained of the number of Shoalers who had relocated to Portsmouth—"In Consequence of which this Town has been burthen'd with the poorer Sort of them since that Time." By 1780, the trade of Portsmouth had declined to 4 percent what it had been before the war, such that "Multitudes are reduced from easy Circumstances, to want & beggary, and half the Inhabitants," which still included the refugees from Gosport, "have frequently been without Bread or Fuel." The town complained that the inflationary cost of poor relief had risen from 30,000 to 80,000 pounds in one year!

One Shoaler who refused to leave the islands during the war was Samuel Haley, who owned Smuttynose Island. Haley had come to the Isles around 1750 and had enjoyed prosperity. He built a simple saltbox home that still stands on Smuttynose. He also constructed a sea wall between Smuttynose and Malaga Island that provided a secure harbor for sailing and merchant vessels. "At one time," antiquarian Samuel Drake wrote, "by his energy, Mr. Haley had made of his island a self-sustaining possession. Before the Revolution, he had built a windmill, salt-works, and rope-walk; a bakehouse, brewery, distillery, blacksmith's and cooper's shops succeeded in the first year of peace—all going to decay within his lifetime." His reputation remained intact among contemporaries, however, even during the low points of the 1770s and 1780s. Dudley Tyng in 1800 described Samuel Haley and his family as "decent in their deportment, and much before the other inhabitants in point of property and morals."

The remaining inhabitants at Gosport, such as they were, turned to a degenerate and profligate way of living, there being no government, no law and order, no pastoral care, only hunger, fear, and desperation. One of the few Shoalers who had the determination and will to better himself when peace was proclaimed in 1783 was John Newton. A fisherman who had been born and raised at Gosport, Newton possessed the awareness that there was a better way of life than that of the Shoalers during the 1780s and 1790s. Few records document John Newton's life. Son of John Newton and Sarah Currier of Gosport, he was baptized by John Tucke on March 20, 1763. It is unclear if and when John's mother and stepfather, Samuel Webber, relocated to a mainland port town during the Revolutionary War. Later in life John Newton seems to have had a special affinity for Newburyport, so perhaps that is where he and his family spent the war. Wherever he was, he learned how to read and write. At some point after the end of the war, Newton married a woman named Sally; they had at least four children. Newton prospered sufficiently that he owned his own dory, or shallop, and made frequent trips to Newburyport to sell his fish. He was quickly emerging in 1790s Gosport as a leader of the reviving town.

Gosport, however, at the end of the eighteenth century was a faint echo of the bustling, noisy fishing port of a generation earlier. Most of the inhabitants

Newburyport on the Merrimack River. *Courtesy of Russell M. Lawson.*

were illiterate, ignorant, depraved and addicted to "ardent spirits, which has been a principal mean of the lamentable degeneracy of these people." Most of the families that inhabited Star Island were "in a state of great poverty and wretchedness." Poverty and wantonness led some of the Shoalers to dismantle the meetinghouse and use the wood for fuel. They were without religion, without instruction, without morality, a "forsaken people." But then John Newton met Dudley Tyng.

Chapter 4

Tyng's Revival

Dudley Atkins Tyng was a fascinating character whose story has never been told by historians. He emerges from the scant historical records as one who was stern yet empathetic, acquisitive but charitable. His son, Captain Charles Tyng, reflecting on his father in a long forgotten yet recently published memoir, *Before the Wind*, portrays the elder Tyng as someone to fear, respect and honor out of duty rather than love without conditions. The father was inflexible with the son, who later recalled the years growing up under tutors and masters, away from home, without pleasure. On the other hand, Dudley Atkins Tyng was a Mason who exhibited the charity and professed benevolence characteristic of that order. In a 1787 publication, Tyng, "Treasurer of St. John's Lodge Newbury-port," argued that Masons must exhibit "a fervent and uniform Love to our Brother; an habitual readiness to evince this Love by extending Relief to him in distress, as far as may lie in our Powers."

Dudley Atkins was born in 1760 to Dudley Atkins Sr. and Sarah Kent Atkins. He was educated at Harvard, studied law and became a practicing lawyer and justice of the peace at Newburyport by the mid 1780s. In 1790 he inherited a small farm on the condition that he adopt the surname Tyng. Dudley Atkins Tyng was one of the backers of what became the Locks and Canals Company of the Merrimack Valley. He married Elizabeth Higginson, the daughter of merchant Stephen Higginson, in 1792; they had eight children. Dudley and Elizabeth Tyng lived on what is today Tyng Street near the wharves and harbor of the small port. Newburyport at the end of the eighteenth century was about forty years old, situated at the mouth of the Merrimack River. Second only to Portsmouth as the leading port north of Boston, Newburyport was a shipbuilding center. The large harbor at the mouth of the Merrimack was a perfect place for sailing craft of all types and sizes to embark and disembark, notwithstanding that a large sandbar, Plum Island, barred part of the entrance to the harbor. Dudley Tyng was involved in community and state affairs, such as the founding of the Massachusetts Historical Society in Boston in 1791. He revealed his interest in history in several published and unpublished documents. One of the latter, in the collections of the Massachusetts Historical Society, is a brief history of Tyng's involvement with John Newton and the inhabitants of Gosport. Tyng wrote:

> *From early life the name of "the Isles of Shoals" had been familiar to me, as a place of resort for invalids, to whom the sea air had been recommended, and for parties of pleasure. I had known many of the inhabitants of the Islands, occasionnally* [sic] *visiting Newburyport for the procuring of salt and other necessaries for carrying on the Fisheries. Many of the children had been placed at service in families, or apprenticed to traders in Newburyport. In this way a frequent intercourse was maintained between the two places. It was here too that the inhabitants sought a market, as well for their* table fish, *which were almost exclusively cured on the Isles of Shoals, as for those other kinds suitable for the European and West India markets. In the Sale of their Fish, these people found a rich reward of their enterprise and industry, being abundantly supplied with the comforts and conveniences of life. This state of things continued until the commencement of the revolutionary war. The exposed and defenceless situation of the islands caused the greater part of the inhabitants to remove to the main, leaving only a few families, who were probably too poor to meet the expense of such an emigration, or of too low a reputation to hope for a welcome in the well regulated societies on the main in their vicinity. From this time all civil order and all moral and religious instruction ceased; and the most deplorable ignorance, with vice in its most disgusting forms, overspread the settlement. In process of time some of the men, more shrewd and more industrious than the rest, began to improve their condition and to grow in some measure sensible of the degraded state of their society, and to wish for its amelioration.*

One of these men was John Newton. Newton and Tyng became acquainted after July 1795, when Tyng "was appointed by President Washington to the office of collector of the customs for the District of Newburyport." Tyng recalled that "the owners of the few small fishing vessels then belonging to the Islands had considered themselves as attached to this district, and had been accustomed, though improperly, to obtain their licenses here" rather than at Portsmouth, customs district of New Hampshire.

When at leisure my curiosity prompted me to converse with these persons on the then state of the Islands. Discoursing one day with Mr. John Newton, who was waiting for his license to be expedited, he percieved [sic] *that I felt some commiseration for him and his miserable neighbours, and earnestly solicited my aid and influence in procuring them some means of improvement.*

As a mason and communicant of St. Paul's Episcopal Church, Tyng was familiar with the work of the Society for Propagating the Gospel among the Indians and Others in North America. He knew of several clergymen involved with that charitable group, such as the Reverend Jedidiah Morse, pastor of the first parish at Charlestown, Massachusetts. Although Tyng was not acquainted with Reverend Morse, and social convention usually required an introduction, he assumed the risk of writing the reverend a long letter introducing himself and requesting Reverend Morse's benevolence in this important matter. Armed with the catalogue of misfortune supplied by John Newton, Tyng wrote:

Newburyport April 27 1799

Rev. & Dear Sir,

Having lately, from the office in which I am here placed, had my attention considerably called to the situation of the people inhabiting the Isles of Shoals; *I am convinced that they are as wretched a little community, as ever excited the charity of man. Confident that no apology will be required by you, for any application in the cause of Humanity and virtue, I shall use the freedom to lay before you such circumstances as are known to me respecting these people. This I shall do to justify my request that you will mention them to your venerable "Society for propagating the Gospel among the Indians and others in North America." And I indulge the hope that such a portion of aid will be extended to them, as, comparing the state of your funds, and of previous appropriations with the suitableness of this object, will appear fit and proper to the Society or its managers.*

These Islands, lying partly in New Hampshire and partly in the district of Maine, are seven in number; two only of which are inhabited. Star Island *contains eighteen families, comprehending ninety souls.* Smutty-nose Island *contains two families, comprehending twelve souls.* Hog-Island, *the largest and containing the most land fit for cultivation, has been wholly uninhabited since the revolution: owing, as I am informed, to an uncertainty in the title.*

Of the whole number of these inhabitants, not more than three or four are possessed of any property, other than the miserable huts which they inhabit. And their deplorable ignorance is not exceeded by their poverty. Perhaps not one fourth part of the people are now able to read; and of these, a very few indeed can write even their names.

Newburyport Harbor. *Courtesy of Russell M. Lawson.*

It is now near thirty years since the death of the Rev. John Tucke, *who was the last, and I believe the only, minister ever settled there. This excellent man, whose memory is yet dear to the elder inhabitants, was their Preacher, their Magistrate, their Schoolmaster and their Physician. His Instructions and his example, promoted Industry, sobriety and Cleanliness, not less than those higher virtues and graces, which form the Christian character.*

All these are now in a Lamentable state of decay. From what I learn, many of the inhabitants are grieved at this state of things; and, not without probable ground, anticipate a decline to the state of savages, in course of a generation or two. They encourage the idea, that if some person, of a character united to their wants, could be induced to fix himself amongst them, some portion of his support might be obtained from the inhabitants. Should one effect (and to me it is not an improbable one) be the increase of industry and exertion, their abilities would increase; and it cannot be doubted that, under proper direction, their inclinations would keep pace with their abilities. Perhaps too occasional, if not permanent, assistance might be obtained from the Government of New Hampshire, could the influence of some leading characters be engaged to the object. A personal friendship, which I hold with two or three of them, should gladly be used as an instrument.

It will readily occur that, for a situation of this kind, no very brilliant talents, or depth of learning, are required. Patience, zeal, diligence, and habitual kindness, are qualities, which want opportunity for continual exercise. These may perhaps be found, where the others are not; and in some person, who would be less desirous of worldly emolument, than of promoting the cause of Religion, Virtue and Good Learning. But I am obtruding observations, which are unnecessary in an address to you.

I will just add, that there is a considerable resort of parties, for health and amusement, to these Islands, from this and other towns on the Main; and that an estimable man, in the situation contemplated, might expect frequent instances of kindness and assistance from this source, as well as occasional relief from the tedium, naturally arising from the ordinary state of society.

Should the patronage of your society be extended to these wretched people, I have good hopes that some aids could be obtained here by private contributions: perhaps enough to set them up a small public building, which should serve as well for a school-house, as for a place of public worship. I promise my utmost exertions to this effect; well assured as I am, that benevolence has very rarely met an object so suitable for its exercise.

I am, Dr. Sir…

Tyng waited four months for a reply from Jedidiah Morse, who was a busy man involved in maintaining the conservative, Puritan way of life at his parish in Charlestown, Massachusetts; promoting his literary works, such as the *American Geography*; involving himself in missionary activities directed toward the Native Americans of upstate New York and beyond and communicating tirelessly with scientists and intellectuals on both sides of the Atlantic. Finally a letter arrived, in which Morse declared the intention of the Society for Propagating the Gospel to provide monetary and spiritual encouragement for a missionary to be sent to Gosport for a three month trial to preach and teach school, and for a new meetinghouse to be built to conduct religious services. Tyng had a chance to briefly meet the missionary, Reverend Jacob Emerson, of Reading, Massachusetts, when he stopped at Newburyport on his way to the Isles to begin his duties.

Tyng, the instigator of Emerson's assignment, was justly curious about how the Shoalers would receive the missionary; he waited for eight days, "supposing that he had then been well settled in his new situation," before Tyng himself "procured a vessel" and set forth to the Isles of Shoals. Tyng hoped to be able to discover Emerson's "first impressions" and to discourse at length with the missionary about what the people of Gosport needed from him.

Tyng journeyed with friends and "other respectable gentlemen" of Newburyport, intrigued with Tyng's benevolent project. On the short voyage to the isles, if the day was clear, Tyng could juxtapose the distant rocky isles with the receding Plum Island and harbor at the mouth of the Merrimack; the Great Boar's Head and Little Boar's Head, land forms protruding from the coast of New Hampshire; and the church spires and white pines of Hampton, the place of Tucke's birth. One imagines the questions that perplexed Tyng, questions that had inspired his journey to Gosport:

How can a people grow so dependent upon one man that upon his death their spiritual, moral and social institutions and behavior descend into "a state of heathenism"?

What was the source of the ongoing affection that the Shoalers continued to extend to this man, long dead?

What in John Tucke's character kindled such powerful devotion?

Upon arriving, Tyng reported, "I there found Mr. Emerson, who had arrived but a few hours before me. Of course I could obtain little information from him. I was pleased to observe that he was not disgusted with the appearances of things about him; and the people seemed gratified at his coming amongst them. He remained some months on the islands, and did what he could. But he was advanced in life, and indeed appeared not to have been originally of great energy of character."

As Tyng's manuscript on the Shoals ends abruptly, it is unknown whether or not he stayed at Gosport for a day or a week. Somehow, he had the energy and resourcefulness to acquire enough information on the natural and human history of as well as the state of affairs on the islands to pen, shortly after his visit, a long *Description and Historical Account of the Isles of Shoals*, which was published in the *Collections* of the Massachusetts Historical Society for 1800. Tyng relied on two sources of information, the town records of Gosport, which he researched and from which he took notes, and local informants, particularly John Newton, who took the visitor on a tour of Star Island (and perhaps the other isles, too), portraying its present condition and describing its recent past.

"There are *eight* Islands in the cluster that bears" the name, Isles of Shoals, Tyng began:

> *compactly situated, viz.* Hog *Island, of about 350 acres;* Star *Island, of about 150 acres;* Haley's *or* Smutty-Nose *Island, or about 100 acres. These are the principal, and the only ones that are habitable. The others are* Cedar, White, Londonners's, Malaga, *and* Duck *Islands; the largest of which contains about eight acres, the smallest one acre. They lie nine miles S.E. of Portsmouth light-house, (NH) and 21 N.E. of the light-houses at Newburyport. N. Lat. 42°. 59'. W. Long. from London, 70°. 30'…The only secure harbour in these islands is Haley's, which opens to the S.W. having Haley's island S.E. Malaga N. W. a wall, built by Mr. Haley, between 70 and 80 paces in length, on the N.E. This little, well sheltered harbour is of great importance, not only to the fishermen of these islands, but to the merchant vessels coming on this coast, who, not infrequently, have been obliged to put into the Shoals, in distress. Many lives and much property have been saved by means of this harbour, and the timely and human exertions of these hardy islanders.*

Fishing for mackerel from a dory. *From photograph by T.W. Smillie. Courtesy of the National Oceanic and Atmospheric Administration.*

"These islands," Tyng continued:

> *have a dreary and inhospitable appearance, and but for their advantageous situation for carrying on the fisheries, would probably never have been inhabited. They are a bed of rocks, raising their disjointed heads above the water. The greater part of their surface is covered with a thick soil, yielding grass sufficient to support, during the summer and autumn, twenty or thirty cows, and about 150 sheep. The sheep raised here are usually killed before winter. Nearly half the sward, on Star Island, has, within a few years, been cut up by the necessitous inhabitants, dried and burnt, instead of more solid fuel. Upon all the islands there are chasms in the rocks, several yards wide, and from one to ten deep, occasioned, if we may judge from appearances, by some violent earthquake. In some places, acres of rock are broken off from the rest of the island; and through the cracks or guts, the water, at high tides and in storms, rushes in torrents.*

Tyng learned that winters at the Shoals were "very bleak," though the weather in summer "is delightfully cool and salubrious." Rarely was there the "need of a physician," as the climate "at all seasons [is] very healthful." Yet at the same time "the inhabitants are not remarkable for longevity," which Tyng blamed on their hazardous occupation. The inhabitants on Star Island held the lands in common, save for the random garden and pasture; a few hardy vegetables and a small amount of hay was the most the land could produce. "A few willows and lombardy poplars, planted by the inhabitants, are the only trees on these islands. Whortle-berries, choak-plums, and a few cranberries, are found on Hog and Haley's isles." There were few wells on the islands, and only one "perennial spring," on Appledore. "The clouds furnish the inhabitants with the greater part of their water for domestic uses."

Tyng was surprised to discover the former prosperity of the islands.

> *For more than a century previous to the revolutionary war, these islands, considering their size and situation, were populous, containing from three to six hundred souls. On Hog island, which is now without an inhabitant, there were between twenty and thirty families, who, in general, were good livers. In so prosperous a state were these islands formerly, that gentlemen, from some of the principal towns on the sea coast, sent their sons here for literary instruction.*

Who the professor was that attracted such a reputation for excellence, Tyng did not learn from his sources.

> *Before the war, when the islands were in a flourishing state, there were annually caught here, and cured for the market, from* three *to* four thousand *quintals of fish. At that time, seven or eight schooners, besides boats, were employed in this business; and some used to extend their fishing voyages to the banks of Newfoundland. About the year 1730, and afterwards, the fisheries on these islands increased to that degree, that three or four ships used to load here, annually, with winter and spring merchantable fish, for Bilboa, in Spain, and smaller vessels for other places.*

On his tour of the islands Tyng could see for himself how the image of prosperity of the past differed from actual misery of the present. "In the autumn of 1800, there were but eighteen families on all these islands, fifteen on Star, and three on Haley's island, containing in all 112 souls" who, "four or five families excepted," are "a miserable set of beings, extremely poor, dirty, and wicked." The inhabitants of Smuttynose, Samuel Haley, "an ingenious and respectable old gentleman…and his two sons, with their families," lived in "three decent dwelling-houses." By contrast, "on Star island, are seven dwelling-houses, if they may be so called. Four excepted, they appear to be, of all abodes of human beings, the most loathsome."

Listening to Newton and other islanders, Tyng heard a verbal portrait of the esteem in which John Tucke was held by the inhabitants. They told Tyng that the Reverend John Tucke was an exceptional man, a fisher of men, one who made his mark among thousands of men and women but in a quiet, anonymous way, without fanfare, seeking the simple reward of service to others in love. Tyng put the impressions into words:

> *These islands, in former times, were in a very respectable and flourishing state. The inhabitants were industrious, prudent, temperate, and regular and decent in their attendance on the institutions of religion. They had magistrates and other officers annually chosen by the people, to execute their wholesome laws and regulations, and to maintain order and peace in the society. The inhabitants were respectful, kind, generous to their minister; and considering the nature of their*

Halibut schooner during summer fishing. *Drawing by Captain J.W. Collins. Courtesy of the National Oceanic and Atmospheric Administration.*

> *employment, and their consequent habits, they dwelt together in a good degree of harmony. Such appears to have been the prosperous and happy state of the inhabitants of these islands, particularly during the ministry of Mr. Tucke. This good man died, deeply and universally lamented, on the 12th of August, 1773; having buried his wife two months before...Mr. Tucke was a man of an affable and amiable disposition, of easy and polite manners, of humble and unaffected piety, of diligence and fidelity in the service of the ministry...In imitation of his Divine Master, he went about doing good among all classes of the people of his charge, and his labours were not in vain in the Lord. Under his nurturing, pastoral care; his people increased in numbers and in wealth, in knowledge, piety and respectability. Few parishes in New-England, at this period, gave a more generous support to their minister, and few congregations were more constant and exemplary in their attendance on public worship. Such is the account of the character of this venerable man, and of the fruits of his labours, which I have received from many aged and respectable people, who were personally acquainted with him.*

Through Tyng's agency, a stone memorial was erected to Reverend Tucke. The epitaph reads:

Underneath
are the Remains of
The Rev. John Tucke, A.M.
He graduated at Harvard College, A.D. 1723.
Was ordained here July 26, 1732,
And died Aug. 12, 1773.
Æt. 72.
He was affable and polite in his manner,
Amiable in his disposition,
Of great piety and integrity, given to hospitality,
Diligent and faithful in his pastoral office.
Well learned in History and Geography, as well as
General Science,
And a careful Physician both to the bodies
and the souls of his People
Erected 1800. In Memory of the Just.

In the wake of Tucke's death, however, Tyng learned that:

> *the laws and regulations, by which their fathers were governed, and which were means of preserving order and harmony in their little commonwealth, were laid aside. The people neglected the annual choice of town officers. They had no regular schools for the education of their children. The sabbath was neglected and profaned. In consequence of these deviations from the "old paths and good ways" of their fathers, the people rapidly degenerated. The vices of cursing and swearing, drunkenness, quarrelling, and disobedience to parents, became, in an awful degree, prevalent. The people have grown up in a great degree ignorant of the great doctrines and duties of religion, and of the first rudiments of science and letters; and, in the near neighbourhood of Christians, were degenerating fast to a state of heathenism.*

Reverend Emerson remained on the islands, holding church and school, for three months, until the onset of winter. The experiment breeding some success, the following summer the Reverend Jedidiah Morse journeyed as agent of the Society for Propagating the Gospel. He arrived August 6, 1800, and stayed for five days, preaching, catechizing and baptizing. He brought for the edification of the islanders "6 bibles, 12 Testaments, 24 Spelling books, 12 Primers, 12 Little Truths, 8 Wall Catechisms, 6 Doddridge's Sermons to young people, 4 Doddridge's Rise and Progress;" Dudley Tyng sent "3 Psalm books." Reverend Morse also included a number of his sermons and a copy of his *Elements of Geography*. He baptized two adults and about thirty children, including the five children of John and Sally Newton. Morse married two couples, both of which had been living together for a decade and had produced a number of children. Thomas Mace "had been formerly married to another woman who had left him, & cohabited with her uncle, by whom she has a number of children. No regular Divorce had been obtained" by Mace. "Considering the peculiar deranged state of the people on these islands," Morse wrote, "& the ignorance of the parties, it was thought expedient, in order as far as possible to prevent future sin, to marry them."

Reverend Morse learned that the people of Gosport and Haley's Island had a desire and commitment to establish a new church, both physical and spiritual. Dudley Tyng solicited donations from "gentlemen of humane feelings and of liberality, in Salem, Newburyport, Portsmouth, Exeter, Ipswich, Boston, Charlestown." The new meetinghouse, measuring thirty-six by twenty-four feet, with thick stone walls and plainly decorated, was quickly erected during September and October. Dudley Tyng was on hand on October 29, 1800, to report that "this day the stone building on the hill is completed and it is intended by the donors to be used as a place of public worship and as a school house and it is hoped it may be useful as a landmark for seamen." Six pews were purchased by the wealthiest locals, including the Mace, Pierce, Haley, Caswell and Newton families. Two weeks later, on November 14, Rev. Morse returned to dedicate the meetinghouse, preaching a sermon from the text of Psalm 118: "O Lord, I beseech thee, send now prosperity." Significantly, he oversaw the parishioners drawing up and pledging to "Articles of Agreement entered into by the Inhabitants of the Isles of Shoals, Nov. 14, 1800."

> *Whereas the islands now commonly called the* Isles of Shoals, *but heretofore named* Smith's Islands, *in honour of the renowned Capt. John Smith, who first discovered them, have fallen into a lamentable state of decay, since the revolution war; and the inhabitants, from their extreme poverty, and other unhappy circumstances, have long been destitute of the means of religious and moral instruction; and whereas some pious and charitable persons have generously erected a commodious and durable building, to be solely appropriated to the public instruction of the inhabitants, and the Massachusetts Society for propagating the gospel have appointed a missionary to reside at the said islands, as a religious and moral teacher to the inhabitants, and an instructor of the youth; and whereas there is ground to hope for further charities from the said society, and other humane and benevolent persons, should the good effects of their present bounty be visible in the improvement of the morals, manners, and conversation of the inhabitants; and whereas from the local situation of the said islands, it is very difficult to resort to the laws for the decision of disputes which unavoidably arise:*
>
> *We the said inhabitants do hereby solemnly and mutually covenant and agree with each other in the following articles, all of which we promise to observe and keep, viz.*

Fully rigged fishing schooner. *Drawing by Captain J.W. Collins. Courtesy of the National Oceanic and Atmospheric Administration.*

A modern schooner with fore and aft rigging. *Courtesy of Benjamin Lawson.*

> First. *We engage to treat with kindness and respect all such worthy and godly persons as shall come to instruct and reform us; to render them as comfortable as we can, and to attend with sobriety and diligence on all their instructions, whether the same be public in the meetinghouse, or private and personal in our own houses.*
>
> Second. *We engage that our children shall also attend the school at the stated hours, and that we will, be setting them sober and good examples, and by needful corrections, labour to make them better, as well as more decent and mannerly in their behaviour.*
>
> Third. *We promise our best endeavours to abstain from all brawling, quarrelling, profane swearing and cursing, drunkenness, idleness, dishonesty, and all other conduct which is offensive to God, and all good beings.*
>
> Fourth. *Should any disputes arise amongst any of us, we promise to submit the same to the decision of the missionary for the time being, and two assessors, who shall be annually chosen in the month of January; and we promise to abide by, and perform their award touching such disputes.*
>
> Fifth. *The house lot and garden, heretofore occupied by the Rev. Mr. Tucke, shall be forever appropriated to the use of the public teacher for the time being.*

This remarkable document, which may remind us of a promise by recalcitrant children to not be naughty again, though doubtless drawn up by Jedidiah Morse, nevertheless has the earmarks of the kind of approach toward faithfulness and goodness that John Tucke spent his life trying to instill in the hearts and minds of the Shoalers. The awareness of history, both the distant past of the founding of their community as well as the recent past of their misbehavior; the willingness to accept love and charity from others and respond in kind and the courage to ask for forgiveness and to make a fundamental change in one's life—such were the core of the teachings of Reverend John Tucke.

Chapter 5

Ebb and Flow

Customs official Dudley Tyng believed that the future of the Isles of Shoals lay in the possibility that the government of the United States would recognize the Isles' historical importance as an outpost of the Atlantic fishery, and establish a "free port," whereby government customs officials and the U.S. Navy would prevent smuggling, develop Gosport into a major port for trade and fishing and perhaps become "an excellent nursery for seamen to man our infant navy." Tyng's dream never came to fruition. Instead, partly because of his efforts in making known to others the beauty of the Isles of Shoals, the Isles grew to become a destination for tourists and those tired in body and soul needing respite from the heat, concerns, and busyness of the mainland cities, such as Boston, Salem, Newburyport, Portsmouth, Portland and beyond. Indeed, even during the dreary years after the conclusion of the War for Independence, the Isles increasingly became "a place of resort for invalids, to whom the sea air had been recommended, and for parties of pleasure."

Notwithstanding apparent tourism at the islands, most of the local inhabitants struggled to make ends meet and lived on the verge of desperation. Men of God such as John Low, who served for a brief time during the winter of 1800 to 1801, and Josiah Stevens, who served the Shoalers from the spring of 1801 to the summer of 1804, worked to fulfill the vision of John Tucke of God-fearing people living upright lives. Stevens was a justice of the peace and practicing minister who married Susanna, the daughter of Samuel Haley Jr., in May 1801. For awhile the couple lived on Smuttynose, where the Haley family lived, until a new parsonage was

Fishing for mackerel in Massachusetts Bay. *From photograph by T.W. Smillie. Courtesy of the National Oceanic and Atmospheric Administration.*

built during the summer and fall. One of Stephens's accomplishments was to encourage and organize the reestablishment of town meetings, which began again in 1803; Stephens served as town clerk and moderator of the town meeting. A more dubious accomplishment was Stephens's successful installation of colonial-style stocks, wooden contraptions to lock up the arms and neck of recalcitrant malefactors. Josiah Stephens died unexpectedly in 1804. His epitaph reads:

In Memory of The Rev. Josiah Stephens,
A faithful Instructor of Youth, and pious
Minister of Jesus Christ.
Supported on this Island by the
Society for Propagating the Gospel,
who died July 2, 1804.
Aged 64 years.

Perhaps because Stephens was town clerk and kept the minutes of the town meetings, after his death the town records of Gosport are silent for twenty-five years. Scattered references to Gosport before 1845, when the town began again to elect officers, come from the records of the Society for Propagating the Gospel as well as other, similar missionary societies. In the spring of 1822, for example, "a theological student," Reuben Moody, journeyed to the Isles to preach and teach. Moody had little success in both endeavors, as his mode of instruction was Draconian, and his preaching dilatory. Moody wrote:

> *Had to leave my school today to drive a scholar into it who was hiding under the rocks and walls. Several people were looking on but I did not administer correction till I had entered the porch and they have nothing to talk about. After this she refused to read and procured another whipping. My scholars have the worst of tempers and will refuse to read if corrected ever so slightly. I find there is no way to deal with them but to make them stand in the greatest fear of me.*

To achieve this goal he used "a short stick" that he "rapped" upon the head of his students. When he asked his students such leading questions as, "what become of wicked children when they die," he "could obtain no answer." Parents would interrupt his sermons with impertinent questions. Alcoholism was rampant and "parents will allow their children to go almost naked and without food in order to satisfy the craving for drink." Another missionary wrote, "he has not the least hope that the benevolent intentions of the Society can ever be thoroughly accomplished till the use of ardent spirits is restrained." Moody was astonished on April 30, 1822, when one man was so intoxicated that he became completely senseless: "Yesterday my heart was shocked at seeing a man about seventy years of age, as devoid of reason as a maniac, giving way to his passions; striving to express himself in more blasphemous language than he had the ability to utter; and, being unable to express the malice of his heart in words, he would *run at* every one he saw."

Besides sickness of the mind there was sickness of the body on the Isles of Shoals, which contradicted the reports of observers and visitors that the climate of the Isles was beneficial to the health—indeed during the 1800s the Isles were increasingly prescribed by physicians as the medicine that might lead to a cure. Celia Thaxter wondered about the ill health and high mortality rate of the islanders, and believed the cause was, ironically, their refusal to allow the healthful sea winds to penetrate their homes. The islanders, she wrote:

> *hermetically sealed their houses, so that the air of heaven should not penetrate within. An open window, especially at night, they would have looked upon as madness,—at temptation of Providence; and during the winter they have deliberately poisoned themselves with every breath…I have seen a little room containing a whole family, fishing-boots and all, bed, furniture, cooking-stove in full blast, and an oil lamp with a wick so high that the deadly smoke rose steadily, filling the air with…"filthiest gloom," and mingling with the incense of ancient tobacco-pipes smoked by both sexes…every crack and cranny was stopped…Shut in that deadly air, a part of the family slept, sometimes all. What wonder their chests were hollow, their faces haggard, and that apathy settled upon them! Then their food was hardly selected with reference to health, saleratus and pork forming two of the principal ingredients of their daily fare.*

Thaxter also reported, in *Among the Isles of Shoals*, that mothers fed their infant children "beans swimming in fat…with the pork cut up in squares," washed down with "bitter-strong black coffee sweetened with molasses."

Reverend Moody was not long for these Isles. At the same time, however, benevolent Christians in Newburyport organized the Society for Propagating Religious Instruction in the Isles of Shoals, which sent missionary Hannah Peabody to the Isles in 1823. According to Rufus Emery:

> *She was very successful in her work. One of her objects was to instruct the people in useful and industrial works and teach them the simple elements of education. On Sundays she read to as many as would come to hear. She visited the people and took special care and oversight of the children, sometimes taking them to her home to keep them from bad parental influence. When the girls were not in school she taught them carding, weaving and netting. One year she reports one hundred and thirty-eight yards of cloth, four hundred and sixteen skeins of yarn, spun by the girls of her school, and sixty by a poor woman; also thirty-three skeins of twine,*

> *one hundred and eighteen yards of netting and chip for twenty hats. The cloth was used to furnish garments for the children of the school, some given to the poor on the islands, and some sold in Portsmouth and Newburyport. This report is a record of her zeal, self-denial and fidelity.*

The editor of the Gosport Town Records, Joseph Warren, recorded other scattered information about Hannah Peabody, that she first came to the Isles in 1821 at the age of nineteen, having "piloted a vessel through the difficult and rocky entrance to the Isles of Shoals." Peabody served at the Isles off and on for eight years before journeying, in 1829, to Chili—she apparently spent much of the rest of her life serving as a missionary in South America. Celia Thaxter wrote that Hannah Peabody:

> *Did wonders for the people during the three years of her stay. She taught the school, visited the families, and on Sundays read to such audiences as she could collect, took seven of the poor female children to live with her at the parsonage, instructed all who would learn in the arts of carding, spinning, weaving, knitting, sewing, braiding mats, etc. Truly she remembered what "Satan finds for idle hands to do," and kept all her charges busy, and consequently happy. All honor to her memory! She was a wise and faithful servant. There is still an affectionate remembrance of her among the present inhabitants, whose mothers she helped out of their degradation into a better life.*

Others answered the call to serve the destitute and ignorant inhabitants of the Isles of Shoals. In 1830 a new meetinghouse was built at the instigation of the Society for Propagating Religious Instruction in the Isles of Shoals. The house was dedicated in September, and the Reverend Leonard Withington of Massachusetts preached the "dedication sermon from Genesis 28: 17 'How dreadful is this place! This is none other but the house of God, and this is the gate of Heaven!'" Subsequently there was a succession of missionaries who taught and preached at the Isles. Portsmouth missionary Clementina Peirce held school during the winter and summer of 1831. "The school consisted of about 30 scholars, between the ages of 2 & 15," representing fifteen families on Star Island. Ms. Peirce taught them "Reading, Writing, Spelling, Defining, Arithmetic, English Grammar, Plain Sewing, &c. The most of them were bright, intelligent children; their improvement was good, generally speaking. They had also the privilege of a Sabbath School which was regularly attended, and interesting." For several years the pulpit and podium were vacant, until in 1834 the Newburyport Society solicited the services of three seminary students—Philip Cleland, Stillman Pratt and Clarindon Muzzy—to spend a short time preaching at the Isles. They stayed at the house and tavern of Joseph Caswell, a fisherman and town leader. There was a spirit of revival during their brief visit. A few months later, in

November 1834, missionary Robert Fuller came to the Isles at the instigation of the Newburyport Society. He preached and taught during the winter, including three sermons every Sunday, and gave addresses on temperance. For several years there is no record of missionaries and teachers serving the islanders until 1837 when the Reverend Origen Smith, of Wilmington, Vermont, came to the Isles. Smith served under the auspices of the Society for Propagating Religious Knowledge for about seven years. Celia Thaxter wrote that Reverend Smith did "much good among the people. He nearly succeeded in banishing the great demoralizer, liquor, and restored law and order. He is reverently remembered by the islanders." About the time that the Reverend Smith was preparing to depart from the islands, another man, a writer and sailor, arrived at Gosport, but not as a missionary or teacher, rather a tourist.

Richard Henry Dana was a graduate of Harvard, a writer and a lawyer who from 1834 to 1836 sailed from Boston to California and back by way of Cape Horn. Dana sailed as a common seaman on two merchant vessels, and wrote a book, *Two Years before the Mast*, published in 1840, based on his experiences. Dana's journey to the Isles began on August 15, 1843, when he took a steamship up the coast from Boston to Portsmouth, passing between the Isles and the mainland. The next day, he hired a boat with the hopeful name of *Temperance*, which was inconsistent with the old salt of a captain named Jackson.

Morning Song

We launch our boat upon the sparkling sea,
We dip our rhythmic oars with song and cheer;
Before our dancing prow the shadows flee,
Behind us fast the fair coasts disappear.
So fade our childhood's shores. Without regret
We leave the safe, green, happy fields, and try
The vague, uncertain ocean, storm-beset,
Nor see the tempests that before us lie.
Flushed with our hope the unknown future gleams,
Freighted with blissful dreams our barque floats on,
And life a shining path of victory seems,
Crowned with a golden peace when day is done.

—*Celia Thaxter*

After negotiating the islands and currents of the Piscataqua, reaching the mouth, and passing Whaleback lighthouse, the captain lay down in the hold to sleep it off, and Dana "took the helm." Upon reaching the northernmost, Duck Island, and knowing the treacherous shoals thereabouts, Dana awakened Captain Jackson and asked for precise directions to avoid shipwreck. They navigated south passing Appledore on the west, sailed "through the channel between Hog and Smutty Nose Islands," where the water was as shallow as three to four fathoms, "and into the cove of Star Island, where he was to leave me." Dana's initial impression was not positive.

> *The prospect was not very encouraging as we walked up to the house where I was to put up. The whole island was less than a mile square, girt with rocks, with very little vegetation and with about twenty painted, weather-stained houses scattered about near the landing-place, without any marks for streets or fences. The whole island had a strong fishy smell, and in going ashore we had to walk over a surface of fishes heads and bones, which the fishermen leave on the beach, just where they throw them, in cleaning.*

Dana put up in the house of Joseph Caswell, captain, fisher, tavern-keeper when guests were about and sometime town clerk (whom Nathaniel Hawthorne a decade later would brand a drunken fisherman), whose house was "the best on the island, and the only one where any company is received." Dana called Caswell "Copwell" in his journal, which is inexplicable until one considers the strange way of speaking of Shoalers. "The real Shoals phraseology," Celia Thaxter wrote in *Among the Isles of Shoals*, "existing in past years was something not to be described; it is impossible by any process known to science to convey an idea of the intonations of their speech, quite different from Yankee drawl or sailor-talk, and perfectly unique in itself. Why they should have called a swallow a 'swallick' and a sparrow a 'sparrick' I never could understand." Hence could "Caswell" sound like "Copwell."

Apprehensive, Dana settled in. The following morning two island boys invited him "fishing in a whaleboat" for "mackerel and haddock." In the afternoon Dana alone took a single-sailed shallop over to White Island. The wind was up, as was the tide and the waves. That evening Dana strolled among the huge rocks of the island, and thought them "the grandest rocks I ever saw" on his many travels. The following morning he again set out alone, this time exploring Appledore and Smuttynose islands. Dana heard from locals that both islands had new owners, named Laighton, "noted rumsellers"—the temperate among the Shoalers feared that the Laightons would "revive intemperance, which has been quite driven out from among the people by means of religious efforts and the total abstinence pledge." Dana came to know Laighton's brother-in-law, Joseph "Cheever, the light-house man," who "seemed to be a clever fellow," and was Laighton's brother-in-law and partner. Dana, Cheever's guest on White Island, eschewed going with Shoalers fishing for hake, partly because "Cheever's boat is a new one, just built, belonging to the government, and a very neat boat and a fast sailer." Cheever "takes great

Fishing for cod on the Grand Banks. *Drawing by H.W. Elliott and Captain J.W. Collins. Courtesy of the National Oceanic and Atmospheric Administration.*

delight in her, and spends hours every day in sailing about among the islands." Cheever unselfishly let Dana take "up the helm," and Dana steered her east, the boat skimming through the water, "the foam flying from her bows." They returned to the Isles and visited Smuttynose, Cheever wanting to introduce Dana to Thomas Laighton, of whom Dana was suspicious because of his questionable reputation and politics—he was reputedly a leader of the radical Democrats (*Locofocos*) in the region. "He was seated on the pier, dressed in the roughest manner, with a coarse, dirty handkerchief about his neck, chewing tobacco and whittling a stick with a jack-knife. There was some thing very unprepossessing about him. He left his seat, and kept on his whittling and chewing as before, and only made an unintelligible sound in answer to Cheever's introduction." Upon conversing with Laighton, Dana discovered "that he had read a good deal, and was a sagacious man, but had strong prejudices and a dislike of established laws and orders, and of any persons who had positions better than his own."

Dana discovered on Saturday that the Shoalers held Saturday evening, and particularly Sunday, as sacred family time. The fishers "cleaned out their boats, took ashore their bait and lines, washed and cleaned themselves and put on clean Sunday clothes, and, the afternoon being pleasant and the breeze good, sailed about in their boats for pleasure. This is the only

Fishing for herring on a schooner in Maine waters. *From a photograph by T.W. Smillie. Courtesy of the National Oceanic and Atmospheric Administration.*

recreation the islands afford, and I am told that they depend upon a pleasant Saturday afternoon to take their families out to sail, and to turn into a pleasure what has been a labor to them during the week." Several generations of families amused themselves sailing about, making port at various islands to explore and to pick berries. Dana later discovered that the Shoalers determined to make the most of Saturday as they could sense a change in the weather coming—the Sabbath day would by stormy. Cheever, who had not lived at the Shoals long enough to engage in or accept such common-sense meteorology, decided that the Shoalers were wrong, so instead of securing his boat at an available cove or harbor, he merely anchored it off White Island. He soon regretted the decision, because the next morning the Shoalers awoke to "a heavy gale from the northeast and the rain beating against the windows." The vessels of the Gosport fishers, secure in their harbor, were safe; not the same could be said for Cheever's boat, "which was pitching at her anchors, the sea breaking outside of her." The people of Gosport stood in the rain, next to the church, watching the boat as it struggled to stay afloat. Dana looked about and observed a "congregation consisted of about twenty-five persons, three or four of whom were hard-favored women, ten or a dozen rough fishermen, and the remainder white-headed and brown-faced boys." The minister, Reverend Smith, who was shallow and unlearned (Dana thought), practically illiterate and anything but an orator, preached on the Second Commandment. Dana thought the "performance" was "flat, wandering, and miserably week." Returning for the afternoon service, Dana "learned that Cheever's boat had swamped close by the rocks on his island, but was kept clear of the rocks by her anchors which still held her." Dana could see the reason for the disaster when he walked down to the shore.

> *The sea was very grand. The long heavy swell set in to the land, forming into high combing seas as it neared the shoaler water, and breaking and rushing up on the steep craggy rock with terrific force and a deafening clamor. I never saw so large seas break on any shore before. They rushed over rocks of the height of forty and fifty feet, and sent their spray far higher into the air. While standing on a high rock, perhaps the highest on the island, and at a distance from its edge which seemed perfectly safe, I was wet through to the skin by an unusually large comber. The swell that set in between Star and Cedar islands was tremendous, and over Cedar Island ledge, which lies about half a mile from the island, the seas broke and threw themselves up into sparkling columns, looking like the fountain in the Park when at its highest play.*

The next day, a Monday, the weather moderated some, the sea not as much, but Dana believed it was sufficiently calm that he could investigate the wreck of Cheever's boat. None of the Shoalers wished to accompany him, as they refused to assist someone in government pay raise a government boat. Dana set off alone—almost, for he took along two landlubbers who volunteered for adventure but knew nothing of boating. Dana sailed close in by the boat; when he saw Cheever disconsolately looking from a rock on White Island, Dana navigated in close to shore, gingerly, until he was close enough, rising and falling with the surf, adjacent to dangerous rocks, to allow Cheever the chance to jump aboard, which he did. Dana let him see the sunken boat, which lay in sufficiently shallow water that he could visually inspect the damage, before conveying him to White Island. Dana returned to Gosport to hear the Shoalers marvel at his seamanship: "one old fisherman said we should be lost, that no boat could land where we did, and when we went under the lee of the ledge, they all thought we had gone over it." Again the Shoalers refused to help Cheever recover the vessel, claiming that if it were his personal (and not government) property, they would help at once. Instead, they went fishing off Cedar Island "to catch mackerel which the northeaster had driven in." Dana "determined to go" in the "same small boat" notwithstanding that "the sea was very high there, and the great rollers came in with such size and force as to make it dangerous and very disagreeable to encounter them in small boats…The rollers were so high and so pitched the boats about that only a quick helm with a stiff breeze kept them from being capsized or swamped." The sea had the boats so completely in its power that they were sometimes "nearly perpendicular," in Dana's view. But then he was admittedly "pitched and tumbled about at such a rate that it completely confused me and made me dizzy, and in a short time I felt sea-sick and vomited a little."

Dana was, by his own account, an accomplished mariner. But he was trying to keep up with the best. Celia Thaxter wrote in *Among the Isles of Shoals* that "to see a *bona fide* Shoaler 'sail a boat'…is an experience:

> *The vessel obeys his hand at the rudder as a trained horse a touch on the rein, and seems to bow at the flash of his eye, turning on her heel and running up into the wind, "luffing" to lean again on the other tack,—obedient, graceful, perfectly beautiful, yielding to breeze and to billow, yet swayed throughout by a stronger and more imperative law. The men become strongly attached to their boats, which seem to have a story of human interest for them,—and no wonder. They lead a life of the greatest hardship and exposure, during the winter especially, setting their trawls fifteen or twenty miles to the eastward of the islands, drawing them next day if the stormy winds and waves will permit, and taking the fish to Portsmouth to sell. It is desperately hard work, trawling at this season, with the bitter wind blowing in their teeth, and the flying spray freezing upon everything it touches,—boats, masts, sails, decks, clothes completely cased in ice, and fish frozen solid as soon as taken from the water.*

Fishing schooner at sea. *Drawing by H.W. Elliott and Captain J.W. Collins. Courtesy of the National Oceanic and Atmospheric Administration.*

Fishing for halibut in the winter. *Drawing by H.W. Elliott and Captain J.W. Collins. Courtesy of the National Oceanic and Atmospheric Administration.*

With the moderate weather of the spring, the fishers would not have to travel so far, as Jeffrey's Ledge, northwest of Duck Island, provided excellent "spring fishing." But the spring brings with it strong gales in which the mariners often found themselves. Celia Thaxter recalled one incident where the fishing fleet was caught in a storm and rather than chance the hazardous route back to Gosport harbor, chose to anchor off the coast of Appledore and ride out the storm. "They were in continual peril; for, had their cables chafed apart with the shock and strain of the billows among which they plunged, or had their anchors dragged (which might have been expected, the bottom of the sea between the islands and the mainland being composed of mud, while all outside is rough and rocky), they would have inevitably been driven to their destruction on the opposite coast." Each fishing schooner was at times perpendicular to the water, and "no one could stand on board of her; the pressure of the wind down on her decks was so great that she shuddered from stem to stern." Meanwhile, "some of the men had wives and children watching them from lighted windows at Star."

"What a fearful night for them! They could not tell from hour to hour, through the thick darkness, if yet the cables held; they could not see till daybreak whether the sea had swallowed up their treasures. I wonder the wives were not white haired when the sun rose and showed them those little specks yet rolling in the breakers!" Fishwives were afraid of the sea, and reluctantly went upon it. Yet every day they watched their fathers, husbands and sons chance fate upon the waters of the Atlantic. "How pathetic, the gathering of women on the headlands, when out of the sky swept the squall that sent the small boat staggering before it, and blinded the eyes, already drowned in tears, with sudden rain that hid sky and sea and boats from their eager gaze!"

Richard Henry Dana, sufficiently humbled by the prowess of the seamen around him, tried to persevere, and "caught several mackerel." Soon it grew so rough that even the Shoalers thought it best to weigh anchor and return to Gosport harbor; Dana gladly followed, but discovered that the wind would not allow a return passage through "Cedar Island passage," between Cedar and Star, but the boats had to proceed southwest and then north around Star Island back to Gosport. On the way, Dana stopped at White to speak with Cheever from his boat, but "the surf was breaking so loud upon the rocks that he could not hear, and so high that it was impossible to land. He made a signal for me to go to lee ward. Here I could communicate with him, but half the words were lost in the roar of the surf." After this futile conversation, Dana returned to Gosport, but the wind and the waves made it difficult; "I beat the little boat over in three tacks, and came safely to moorings before night."

The next morning the fishers prognosticated several days of rain, which determined Dana to return to Portsmouth. He paid his bill to Caswell, and

Schooner fighting a winter storm at the Grand Bank. *Drawing by H.W. Elliott and Captain J.W. Collins. Courtesy of the National Oceanic and Atmospheric Administration.*

declared himself "satisfied with my stay and the treatment I had received." The returning passenger packet also carried Reverend Smith and his daughters. "The parson appeared better in the boat than in the pulpit, though but indifferent here" as well.

Returned from his journey, Dana sat to pen his reflections on the Isles of Shoals:

> *The group called the Isle of Shoals* [he wrote] *consists of seven islands. These are mere beds of rock with spots of vegetation here and there. Two of them, Duck Island and the Londoner's, are not inhabitable, being mere rocks, upon which ducks and sea-birds alight, and to which fishermen make fast their nets. White Island, on which the light-house stands, is also little else than a steep rock with a single patch of soil about the keeper's house. It would not sustain more than one goat from its own produce. A fourth island, called Cedar, is not inhabited, and although I did not land upon it, yet my impression is that it is hardly, if at all habitable. The remaining three, which are the largest, have always had a population upon them. Of these, the largest and most fertile is Hog Island. Smutty Nose, or Smotinose, as it is spelled in the old MS. records, or Smyna, which tradition says is its proper name, is the second in size and fertility. Star Island, so-called from its shape, being nearly circular, with rock projections, is now the most populous, and has always had as much prosperity as any of them. At the present time its entire population is one hundred and fourteen souls. On*

> *Hog Island there are but two houses, recently built by the Leightons* [sic], *who mean to make it their headquarters. Smutty Nose has about half a dozen houses, in a decayed condition, and a population of about twenty souls. It seems likely to be soon deserted. Before the War of the Revolution these islands enjoyed great prosperity. Their fisheries were very profitable, and they afforded security from the attacks of the Indians who molested the people on the mainland. In 1730 the population of the group was eleven or twelve hundred. Hog Island had six hundred of them, Smutty Nose and Star dividing the remainder. There was a good deal of property, many men of influence in the State, physicians, lawyers, a well-paid clergyman, and men of different trades and mechanical arts. The war opened a new danger against which the islands were unprotected. This, together with the decline of the fisheries and the removal of fear from Indian incursions, soon reduced the prosperity of the Shoals. I do not know how low they got, but have an impression that the entire population has been as little as eighty or ninety souls. Some twenty years ago there was a good deal of money made on the islands by three men of the name of Haley, Newton, and Copwell* [Caswell], *the former living on Smutty Nose, and the others on Star. They were reputed to be worth from $10,000 to $30,000 apiece; but the other inhabitants were quite poor and intemperate and indebted to these three. The Haleys ran out their property and have disappeared. The descendants of Newton and Copwell* [Caswell] *still live on Star Island, but their property is all gone, and they labor as common fishermen. There are two or three houses on Star and one on Smutty Nose which look as though they might have been inhabited by people somewhat above the class of day fishermen, but excepting these signs, and the decent gravestones of the Haleys, Newton and Copwells* [Caswells], *and of one or two clergymen, I saw nothing to indicate a previous population. Indeed, I could hardly credit the story that these islands had supported so many persons, and should not but upon the best authority. They must have imported all their wood and nearly all their hay and vegetables. There is a tradition, too, that a school flourished on Hog Island at which the sons of men of fortune in Boston and other parts of the main land were fitted for college. The inhabitants have very much improved in their moral condition within the last three years. Temperance has spread among them, and no ardent spirits are allowed upon Star Island. Drunkenness was unknown there the last year. It is said that the Leightons mean to sell spirits. If they do there will be a fierce contest, for either they or the islanders will be broken up by it.*

Two years after Dana's visit, in 1845, Gosport was resurrected as a town, largely through the work of the Reverend Abraham Plummer, who served the fishers and fishwives for four years, from 1844 to 1848. As there were no town officers, Shoalers led by Reverend Plummer approached Rockingham County (New Hampshire) Justice of the Peace Albert Hatch to call a town meeting. Hatch did so, explaining "that no annual or legal meeting of said…Town has ben holden since the year of our Lord one Thousand

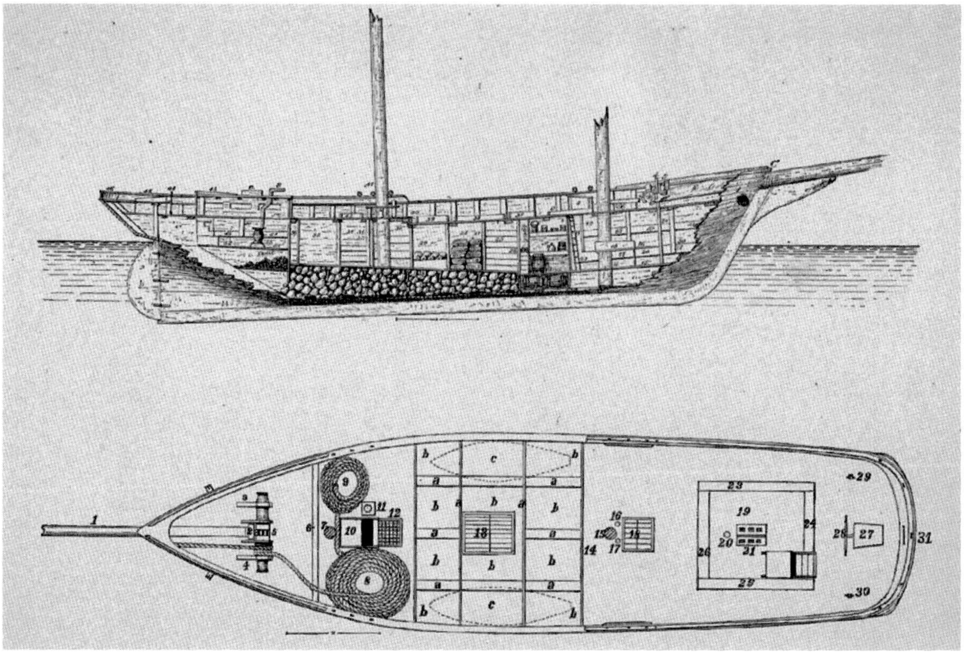

Plans of a nineteenth-century fishing schooner. *Drawings by Captain J.W. Collins. Courtesy of the National Oceanic and Atmospheric Administration.*

Eight Hundred and four." As there was no town constable, who according to New Hampshire law was the local official to warn inhabitants of a town meeting, Hatch appointed Joseph Caswell to perform this office. At this first meeting held in forty years, citizens elected men to the traditional offices of New England towns, such as clerk, selectmen, moderator, constable and tax collector, as well as a new one, harbor master. At the next town meeting in November, the fishers chose a representative to the New Hampshire legislature, and elected men for more new offices—overseer of the poor and highway surveyor. It is difficult to imagine the new surveyor, Asa Caswell, having much work on Star Island; the new overseer of the poor, however, Reverend Plummer had his work cut out for him. At the March 1847 meeting, in addition to the election of constables, townsmen elected three police officers, which reveals an attempt to conform Gosport to changes happening in other towns and cities in America. Two years later, the town voted to purchase "a Boat to be kept by the Town for the express purpose of going to and from the Main for the purpose of getting the Doctor or carrying one who may be sick." Plummer by this time had left Gosport, and perhaps he took with him his physician as well as many other skills that would henceforth be sorely missed. A brief memorial of his services in the town records cites Plummer as being responsible for the construction of a schoolhouse and repairs to the parsonage; "he did most of the work himself," and paid for some expenses out of his own pocket. About a month after Reverend Plummer's departure, the schoolteacher, Miss N.J. Underhill, was killed in an accident. It was one of those days in the wake of a storm of pounding waves and massive breakers that crash, sometimes unexpectedly, upon the shore. Miss Underhill stood too close upon a rocky perch, when a massive wave crashed down upon her, and sucked her into the sea. Her body was recovered a week later off Cape Neddock in Maine. Miss Underhill was in her early thirties.

The departure of Reverend Plummer and death of Miss Underhill left the Isles destitute of a force for thought and change; the town clerk, William Newton, was at least tolerably literate, unlike many others before him in the same office. The replacement for Reverend Plummer, Reverend L.D. Blodgett, served briefly, "when it became manifest to his imployers that for lack of interest in his labors he could accomplish no good among the people." Reverend Blodgett's time on the Isles made the Shoalers look back wistfully upon some of the previous missionaries who had filled the pulpit and schoolhouse. They resolved to find a more suitable man of the cloth, and enlisted the aid of the Society for Propagating the Gospel. The town wrote to Reverend A.P. Peabody of Portsmouth, who had taken an active concern in Gosport affairs for many years. "Although we may not always have appreciated as we ought to have done," the town wrote by way of confession, "their acts of kindness, we will hereafter if our privileges may

Fishing with line for halibut aboard a fishing schooner. *Drawing by H.W. Elliott and Captain J.W. Collins. Courtesy of the National Oceanic and Atmospheric Administration.*

Preparing bait on a fishing schooner. *Drawing by H.W. Elliott and Captain J.W. Collins. Courtesy of the National Oceanic and Atmospheric Administration.*

be continued Set a higher value upon and make a better improvement of them." Perhaps as a sign of good will, the town met in March 1851, and "voted against the Sale of Spirituous liquors in the Town."

The Society for Propagating the Gospel responded to the promises and actions of the people of Gosport by appointing a new missionary, Oliver D. Eastman, to serve the Shoalers. Eastman, of Kingston, began his position in May 1851, and "generally had three meetings on the Sabbath when his health and the weather would permit, and some evening meetings during the week." Eastman's dedication to his charges, both adults and children, made his church and school the most active and well attended in years. The children participated in summer, winter and spring school sessions as well as a "Sabbath-school," learning the rudiments of scripture, reading, writing, arithmetic, geography and astronomy—the latter, at least for the boys, of particular necessity for their future vocation. The citizens of Newburyport, still actively engaged in helping the Shoalers, donated books, maps, a dictionary, a bell and religious pamphlets. Reverend Peabody of Portsmouth gave his advice and blessings. No less than the governor of New Hampshire visited the school. Schoolmaster Eastman reported that

Newburyport Harbor. *Courtesy of Russell M. Lawson.*

> *There was a summer school of twelve weeks commencing June 16th and ending September 13th 1851. The whole number of scholars was 28, males 14 and females 14—Average attendance 18. The irregularity of the scholars attendance injures the school very much...The winter school commenced Nov. 10, 1851, and continued 17 weeks ending March 8th 1852. Whole number of scholars 35. Average attendance 23. Number of scholars under 16 years of age 26. Number of scholars over 16 years of age 9...The improvement in the several branches taught has been very good considering previous opportunities & privileges being very limited. It is very desirable that a greater interest be had in the subject of education. Truly it is the great stepping stone to usefulness in this world and gives us strength of mind to labor for the interest of the world to come.*

Eastman was not only an able teacher but an inspiring preacher as well. There was a revival of sorts on the Isles during the first winter he was present. Many Shoalers "were reclaimed from a backsliding state and expressed their resolution to serve the Lord the remainder of their life. May the Lord bless them and help them to gain *eternal* life."

As happy dwellers by the seaside hear
In every pause the sea's mysterious sound,
The infinite murmur, solemn and profound,
Incessant, filling all the atmosphere,
Even so I hear you, for you do surround
My newly-waking life, and break for aye
About the viewless shores, till they resound
With echoes of God's greatness night and day.
Refreshed and glad I feel the full flood-tide
Fill every inlet of my waiting soul;
Long-striving, eager hope, beyond control,
For help and strength at last is satisfied;
And you exalt me, like the sounding sea,
With ceaseless whispers of eternity.

—*Celia Thaxter*

Chapter 6

Hawthorne's Search

The westerlies skimmed across the peaks and valleys of the rolling waves, prodding the whitecaps toward land. The Norwegian captain of the *Fanny Elsler*, a small ketch that made the daily journey from Piscataqua harbor to the Isles of Shoals and back, cursed the winds, knowing the six-mile voyage was going to be a long one. He steered the ketch into the wind north by west. The billowing sails, fore and aft, strained at the ropes. It was a bumpy ride—the frigid seawater sprayed the few passengers. The hardy ones nevertheless found the breeze invigorating and were thankful for the cloudless day.

The land astern rose and fell with the ship according to the mariner's gaze. The sand of the beach sparkled against a backdrop of tall pine trees. Further inland one spied distant clouds and the White Mountains—though what was cloud and what was hill could scarcely be determined. The bright blue of the sea otherwise enveloped the boat, which struggled against the elements of wind and current. The ketch was helpless against the fathomless depths, the power of nature. The passengers sensed their dependence upon the eternal and infinite, and said silent prayers for redemption and peace.

The ketch appeared to be bobbing up and down, held stationary by the rise and fall of the sea. The appearance in time of distant dark protrusions on the horizon revealed the boat's slow progress toward a destination. These anomalies amid sameness grew to be jagged and rounded rocks jutting from the sea. The water thereabouts was shoal, demanding careful seamanship.

On this day, September 3, 1852, the wind was cool and the spray cooler. The captain and mate of the *Fanny Elsler* conveyed six passengers toward their destination of the Isles of Shoals. Several of the passengers grew sick in the rough seas; one, a shopkeeper from Danvers, Massachusetts, became violently ill. His traveling companion, also from Massachusetts, as well as a cultured young man from Greenland, a small town next to Portsmouth in New Hampshire, carried on cheerfully notwithstanding the groans of the sick. The captain merrily puffed on cigars as he manned the tiller. Another passenger, inquisitive and observant, a writer on vacation, kept mental notes of the proceedings that he proposed to record later in his journal. Nathaniel Hawthorne was forever observing and writing, fascinated by the whims and actions of his fellow humans. He was between projects, having just finished *The Blithedale Romances* as well as a campaign biography of his friend Franklin Pierce (who was running as the Democratic nominee for the presidency) and preparing to write *Tanglewood Tales*. He sought the rest and refreshment offered by the late summer climate at the Isles of Shoals, and expected to enjoy the society of Pierce and other gentlemen and ladies during his stay.

The voyage took over three hours due to the wind and waves. Upon arriving, the captain navigated the boat for the harbor, a secure refuge from the waves and wind formed between the three largest islands, Appledore, Smuttynose and Star. The passengers disembarked at the boat landing on Appledore, where Thomas Laighton's Appledore House provided accommodations for visitors and tourists. Laighton had built his hotel in 1847 with the help of his partner and son-in-law Levi Thaxter. Hawthorne's arrival was expected, as word of the anticipated Pierce entourage had preceded him to Appledore House. The old gentleman Thomas Laighton welcomed Hawthorne to his hotel, which was a large, several-story building with a promenade and veranda. The sea air swept through the latter, bringing the best refreshment on hot summer days. Laighton introduced Hawthorne to Thaxter, who would be his companion and friend during the next fortnight.

Thomas Laighton had brought his family from Portsmouth to the Isles in 1839. For eight years he, his wife and their three children lived on White Island, a small rocky isle in the sea. "His life there must have been a rough one," Frank Stearns wrote in *Sketches from Concord and Appledore*. "Of all the Isles of Shoals, White Island is the most difficult of access. It is not easy to land there in good summer weather, and during winter communication with the outer world is as rare as cold days in July. From December till May the breakers thunder on the cliff beneath the light-house like the roar of artillery."

Hawthorne's writings reveal his fascination with New England history, an interest he immediately pursued upon arrival at the Isles. Thaxter, acting as guide, took the writer to various sites on Appledore, such as a monument of stones, or cairn, reputedly built by Captain John Smith during his brief stop in 1614. There were the remains of cellars and foundations of homes from

Mackerel fishing. *Drawing by H.W. Elliott and Captain J.W. Collins. Courtesy of the National Oceanic and Atmospheric Administration.*

centuries before, and Hawthorne speculated that one, perhaps, was where William Pepperrell Sr.—the father of the conqueror of Louisburg in 1745 and later leading inhabitant of Kittery, Maine—lived when he first came to America in the late 1600s. The landscape of the island, the bald rock interspersed with mosses and grasses, intrigued Hawthorne, particularly a massive gorge amid the rock of the shore that appeared to one with so gifted an imagination as a perfect cove for pirates looking for a temporary hideout.

His first full day on the islands, September 4, Hawthorne took the daily ferry that went from Appledore to Star Island, accompanied by his two fellow travelers of the day before, brothers who hailed from Massachusetts. They were talkative, asking the boatman numerous questions, and jovial. One, the shopkeeper, was slight and handsome; the other, a farmer, was thickset and had manners like a bumpkin, though he was good-natured. Hawthorne recorded in his journal that Star Island was the most populated of the islands, the site of the town of Gosport. Unlike most New England towns, which had houses lined regularly along cobblestone lanes, the houses of Gosport lacked regularity. Hawthorne wrote that there was not the "slightest…pretence of a street," though oddly the town elected a surveyor of highways in 1845 and in 1854 the townsmen instructed the selectmen "to keep our highways about our public landings free from all unnecessary incumbrances." No doubt they meant the highway of sea lanes. At any rate,

Hawthorne saw neither carriages nor wagons on the rocky isle. The island (naturally) reeked of fish, catching which was the primary livelihood of the inhabitants. A small hotel amid the small fishing houses, some of two-stories, offered refreshment to thirsty travelers. A small, square stone church with a wooden bell tower possessed the highest spot on the island. Hawthorne queried a fisherman, asking who was the clergyman who occupied the pulpit here. The fisherman pointed out "the good man himself, in his suit of black, which looked in a very decent condition at the distance from which I viewed it. His clerical air was quite distinguishable; and it was rather curious to see it, when every body else wore red-baize shirts and fishing boots." Hawthorne learned that the minister and schoolteacher was Oliver Eastman, who had come to Gosport in 1851 sponsored by the Society for Propagating the Gospel, which had charitably involved itself in the affairs of the Isles for half a century. On this brief initial visit to Gosport, Hawthorne "saw one old witch-looking woman, creeping about with a cane, and stooping down, seemingly to gather herbs. On mentioning her to Mr. Thaxter, after my return, he said that it was probably the 'bearded woman.' I did not observe her beard; but, very likely, she may have had one."

Celia Thaxter in *Among the Isles of Shoals* painted a brief portrait of such a woman:

> *Sad, anxious lives they have led, especially the women, many of whom have grown old before their time with hard work and bitter cares, with hewing of wood and drawing of water, turning of fish on the flakes to dry in the sun, endless household work, and the cares of maternity, while their lords lounged about the rocks in their scarlet shirts in the sun…I never saw such wrecks of humanity as some of the old women of Star Island, who have long since gone to their rest. In my childhood I caught glimpses of them occasionally, their lean brown shapes crouching over the fire, with black pipes in their sunken mouths, and hollow eyes, "of no use now but to gather brine," and rough, gray, straggling locks: despoiled and hopeless visions, as if youth and joy could never have been theirs.*

Levi Thaxter had been at the islands for several years, preparing (he claimed) for an acting career, investing in Thomas Laighton's hotel, even serving briefly as Gosport minister. As tutor to the Laighton children, he had fallen in love with the teenage Celia Laighton and had married her when she was but sixteen. To Thaxter's home Hawthorne repaired his first night for conviviality, drinking apple toddy, singing and gazing upon the beautiful Mrs. Thaxter, whom Hawthorne believed was "eighteen years old, very pretty, and with the manners of a lady—not prim and precise, but with enough of freedom and ease." Hawthorne noted that her reading interests, at least by the looks of the table in her "neat little parlor," centered on "Spiritual mediums & c." Later, when the group of young men and women, which included other guests besides Hawthorne, sang "some glees and negro melodies," Hawthorne thought Mrs. Thaxter "sang like a bird."

The future poet and prose writer Celia Laighton Thaxter had lived on the Isles of Shoals since she was four years old, which had formed her mind for reflection and romance. "If it were ever intended that a desolate island in the deep sea should be inhabited by one solitary family," her friend Annie Fields wrote, "then indeed Celia Thaxter was the fitting daughter of such a house." Thaxter's *Among the Isles of Shoals*, when it was published twenty years later, was a literary tonic, as it were, for the loneliness and sameness of the Isles. "The best balanced human mind is prone to lose its elasticity and stagnate, in this isolation," she wrote from experience. "One learns immediately the value of work to keep one's wits clear, cheerful, and steady; just as much real work of the body as it can bear without weariness being always beneficent, but here indispensable." Especially during winter, when the seas are high and the wind strong. "After winter has fairly set in," Thaxter wrote, "the lonely dwellers at the Isles of Shoals find life quite as much as they can manage, being so entirely thrown upon their own resources that it requires all the philosophy at their disposal to answer the demand."

When Hawthorne retired for the evening with thoughts of mirth and the "pretty youthfulness of woman," he strolled to the hotel with his rocky path lit by a "three-quarters waning moon" accompanied by "the old sea moaning all round about the island."

Monday, September 6, Franklin Pierce accompanied by a party of ladies and gentlemen arrived aboard the packet ship *Spy*. After dinner Hawthorne led them across the harbor to Gosport, where they wandered about the graveyard, looking at the old burial places of inhabitants of the past, such as the Reverend John Tucke. Seeking information about the town and its past, the party approached the town clerk, Joseph Caswell. Although Thaxter had told Hawthorne that the intemperate ways of the inhabitants had largely been abandoned, Caswell was "very drunk…He was dressed in the ordinary fisherman's style, red baize shirt, trowsers tucked into large boots, which (as he had just come ashore) were wet with salt-water." Caswell, who was a town leader and sometimes selectman, took them on a tour of the island, showing the wonderful and the miraculous, such as Betty Moody's Hole, where a frightened mother hid with her children during a Native American attack; Miss Underhill's Chair, where the local schoolteacher was swept from her rocky perch into the sea; gigantic fissures in the rock that the locals thought occurred at the Crucifixion; possible locations of buried pirate treasure; and, what intrigued Hawthorne most, the town and church records of eighteenth-century Gosport.

Hawthorne spent some of his days in solitary communion with nature, listening to the surf, watching the gulls, keeping his eye out for the packets from Portsmouth or Newburyport, wandering amid the shrubs and rocks of Appledore Island. "The surface of this island," he wrote:

> *is plentifully overgrown with huckle-berry, and bay-berry bushes. The sheep eat down the former, so that few berries are produced; the latter gives a pleasant fragrance, when pressed in the hand. The island is one great ledge of rock, four hundred acres in extent, with a little soil strewn scantily over it, but the bare rock everywhere emerging, not only in points, but still more in flat serries. The only trees, I think, are two that Leighton has been trying to raise in front of the hotel, the tallest of which looks scarcely so much as ten feet high.*

In the evening the surf pounding the rocks and sandy shores of Rye and Hampton could be heard in the otherwise still of dusk. The next morning broke "sunny and calm…the slightest breeze to the westward; a haze sleeping along the shore, betokening a warm day; the surface of the sea streaked with smoothness, and gentle ruffles of wind." On this hot day Hawthorne strolled over to Smith's monument for a careful look. Hawthorne examined the old stones covered with ancient lichens formed into a rustic cairn. The mass bespoke antiquity, so Hawthorne believed that perhaps Smith did erect it on his visit to the islands in 1614. During the afternoon Hawthorne observed more closely Laighton's hotel, noting that it occupied a slight valley that stretched across the island. Upon inquiry, Hawthorne learned that once a large swell had passed through the valley, dividing the island in half. During the course of his visit, Hawthorne learned from the oldest inhabitants that their fathers and grandfathers recalled a time when at high tide the island was divided in half, and fishing boats put in to unload their catch. In the afternoon a rarity occurred when a shark appeared, swimming just a few feet off the rocky shore. Laighton's son, Oscar, attempted to kill it with a gunshot, without visible success. Laighton told Hawthorne that he had often seen whales about the islands, on one occasion a school of the creatures feeding in the plentiful waters of the Gulf of Maine.

The following day, a Thursday, Thaxter and Hawthorne rowed a dory over to White Island, the southernmost island, a small rocky outcrop that hosted the one lighthouse of the Isles of Shoals. The keeper of the lighthouse lived, reputedly alone, on the lonely isle, with a small house adjoining the stone lighthouse, which was built on a rise of irregularly placed rocks. A triangular-shaped passageway connected house and lighthouse. This island could be battered unmercifully during winter storms, which was reflected in the demeanor of the lighthouse keeper, whom Hawthorne perceived had "a sneaking kind of a look, and does not bear a very high character among his neighbors." Thaxter informed Hawthorne that the keeper had been married twice, the first having died, the second having run away; the keeper took to drinking for solace. Hawthorne believed he heard a woman's voice in the house, as they traversed the island inspecting the keeper's garden of onions, turnips and squash. Returning to Star Island by way of Londoner's Rock, they stopped briefly at this heap of stones without inhabitants save fowl, including white owls and rats.

The Isles betrayed the frequent inconstancy of its weather the next day, a Friday. The day dawned sunny, calm and beautiful, "the sea dimpling in the sunshine," the morning weather prognosticating another sultry day interspersed with fresh sea breezes. Indeed it was such a day for several hours until mid-morning, when the wind changed from the west, the warm zephyrs bringing the heat of the mainland, to the east, a cool wind from across the sea, bringing with it a large bank of fog. The fog was cool and wet, moistening skin and clothing, blocking the rays of the sun, and hiding boats at sea, the mainland shore and surrounding islands. After noon the fog dissipated, though cloudy skies remained. Locals predicted a storm was coming, though it never did, and Hawthorne concluded, "the weather-seers know not what to forebode." By nightfall the fog returned, as did mosquitoes, which "are certainly a hardier race" on the islands "than their inland brethren."

The next day was still cloudy when Hawthorne and Thaxter rowed the short distance to Smuttynose, a long and narrow island situated between Appledore and Star, southeast of the former and northeast of the latter. The island had few inhabitants, there being but a hotel and two dwellings. Morning entertainment was provided by a sloop that, having taken on water the previous day, had been abandoned by the crew, who fled to Smuttynose for help. The inhabitants responded by rowing about, picking up cargo that had floated away from the boat, and rigging it sufficiently to get the partially drowned sloop to shore, where its wet cargo was unloaded. The sloop, according to Hawthorne, was "a black, ugly, rotten old thing, with the water half-way over her deck. The wonder was how she swam so long." The unnamed captain Hawthorne described as "a man of about thirty-five or forty, in a blue pilot-cloth overcoat, and a rusty, high-crowned hat, jammed down over his brow." He put in for "a crop of comfort" at the Smuttynose hotel, appropriately called the Mid-Ocean House of Entertainment, run by Captain Fabius Becker, an old Prussian soldier, now landlord. Hawthorne, fascinated by the captain of the sloop, watched him carefully—"I know not why, but there was something that made me smile in his grim and gloomy mien, his rusty, jammed hat, his rough and grisly beard, and in his mode of chewing tobacco, with much action of the jaws, getting out the juice as largely as possible, as men always do when disturbed in mind. I looked at him earnestly, and was conscious of something that marked him out from among the careless islanders around him" Being as much discomposed as it was possible for him to be, his feelings individualized the man, and magnetized the observer.

Fishing the waters off Cape Anne. *From photograph by T.W. Smillie. Courtesy of the National Oceanic and Atmospheric Administration.*

Hawthorne was similarly intrigued by the natural and human history of Smuttynose Island. "I have never seen," Hawthorne proclaimed about the easternmost point of the island, "a dismaller place than it was in this sunless and east-windy day, being the furthest point out into the melancholy sea, which was in no very agreeable mood, and roared sullenly against the wilderness of rocks." These rocks had been tossed "to and fro" by the "omnipotent" sea—one rock in particular was "twelve feet square…thrown up out of the sea, in a storm, not many years since." Smuttynose had some fertile soil that yielded grass for livestock and beautiful wildflowers, such as the bayberry. There was sufficient soil for graves as well. Smuttynose had many—some of the Haley family, once the owners of the island. Then there was a large grave plot bounded by "rough, mossgrown pieces of granite," containing the remains of sixteen Spanish mariners who had died on the night of January 14, 1813. The ship was a large one of over three hundred tons burden, out from Cadiz in Spain, which got caught in a violent winter storm, east of Smuttynose, driven by the cold east wind upon the rocks of the island. The ship was destroyed and the men died quickly. The Gosport town records called the ship *Sagunto*, though Samuel Haley, the man who found and buried the Spaniards, called it the *Conception*. Laighton told Hawthorne that some of the bodies were found on the island of Malaga, a small isle adjacent to Smuttynose to the west.

The Spaniards' Graves At The Isles Of Shoals

O Sailors, did sweet eyes look after you
The day you sailed away from sunny Spain?
Bright eyes that followed fading ship and crew,
Melting in tender rain?
Did no one dream of that drear night to be,
Wild with the wind, fierce with the stinging snow,
When on yon granite point that frets the sea,
The ship met her death-blow?
Fifty long years ago these sailors died:
(None know how many sleep beneath the waves:)
Fourteen gray headstones, rising side by side,
Point out their nameless graves, —
Lonely, unknown, deserted, but for me,
And the wild birds that flit with mournful cry,
And sadder winds, and voices of the sea
That moans perpetually.
Wives, mothers, maidens, wistfully, in vain
Questioned the distance for the yearning sail,
That, leaning landward, should have stretched again

White arms wide on the gale,
To bring back their beloved. Year by year,
Weary they watched, till youth and beauty passed,
And lustrous eyes grew dim and age drew near,
And hope was dead at last.
Still summer broods o'er that delicious land,
Rich, fragrant, warm with skies of golden glow:
Live any yet of that forsaken band
Who loved so long ago?
O Spanish women, over the far seas,
Could I but show you where your dead repose!
Could I send tidings on this northern breeze
That strong and steady blows!
Dear dark-eyed sisters, you remember yet
These you have lost, but you can never know
One stands at their bleak graves whose eyes are wet
With thinking of your woe!

—*Celia Thaxter*

Sabbath day, September 12, was stormy, what Laighton called "half a gale." The wind and rain blew in from the east; the sea rose and fell and whitecaps were ubiquitous; the surf crashed against the rocky islands—Hawthorne mentioned particularly Square Rock, which lies southwest of Londoner's Island. The sublimity and majesty of the sea pounding the small, isolated Isles captured his imagination, to which he gave vent in his journal. Star and Smuttynose took the largest share of the sea's wrath, so that the waves were less menacing to the shores of Appledore. The gray of the day mixed with the spray of waves and the gale-force winds driving the rain amid the creases of the massive rocks of the Isles elicited from Hawthorne an exclamation of wonder that he put into prose:

> *It is quite impossible to give an idea of the roughness of these rocky shores; how confusedly they are tossed together, lying in all directions; what solid ledges, what great fragments thrown out from the rest. Often the rocks are broken square and angular, so as to form a kind of staircase, though, for the most part, such as would require a giant stride to ascend. Sometimes, a black, trap rock runs through the bed of granite; sometimes, the sea has eaten this away, leaving a long irregular fissure. In some places…there is a great hollow place, excavated into the ledge, and forming a harbor, into which the sea flows; and while there is foam and fury at the entrance, it is comparatively calm within. Some parts of the crag are as much as fifty feet of perpendicular height; down which you look, a bare and smooth descent, at the base of which is a shaggy margin of sea-weed. But it is vain to try to express this confusion; as much as anything else, it seems as if some*

> *of the massive materials of the world remained superfluous, after the Creator had finished, and were carelessly thrown down here, where the millionth part of them emerge out of the sea, and in the course of thousands of years, have got partially bestrewn with a little soil.*

With the close of day the gale ceased, the wind changed, blowing from the west, and the rays of the fading sun appeared. Hawthorne spent the evening with Thaxter and his wife Celia, who was intrigued by the magical and supernatural, as was Hawthorne. They spoke particularly of ghosts, of which the Isles of Shoals had quite a few. One, "a little old woman, in a striped gown," had haunted the Thaxter house once, several months before, but was seen only by their maidservant. More familiar and regular in his haunting was Old Babb, a pirate who had died in the 1600s and was a frequent apparition on Appledore. The islanders said that Old Babb "has a ring round his neck; and is supposed either to have been hung, or to have had his throat cut; but he steadfastly declines telling the mode of his death. There is a luminous appearance about him, as he walks. His face is pale, and very dreadful."

The morning of Monday, September 13, the atmosphere was clear and Hawthorne could see the shores of New Hampshire and Maine, the long sandy beaches of the former, the mansions and church steeples of Portsmouth and Kittery, and Mount Agamenticus in Maine, inland a few miles from the town of York. Further inland Hawthorne could make out the White Mountains. Hawthorne made his way to the southern and southeastern parts of the island, where he discovered the foundations of old stone homes, walls enclosing old gardens and pastures, and long-abandoned cellars. The thought of the inhabitants of two centuries before was singular, and Hawthorne looked about him to see what these long-dead islanders saw so many years before: Star and Smuttynose stood in front across a narrow band of water; between them lay the small Cedar Island, the namesake of small evergreens that perchance once covered the island. The mainland sandy beaches were to the right; Duck Island was in the distance to the left. Great chasms in the rock greeted his eyes and amazed him as they did the islanders of the past. He observed in these chasms the old rocks and interstices formed ages before; weeds and wildflowers that grew year upon year and aged lichens that covered the granite from a time long past. The sea moved in and out of the chasm in eternal regularity.

The next day, September 14, Hawthorne prepared to depart; he packed his belongings, though the opportunity to leave for Portsmouth did not present itself for two days. In his luggage Hawthorne carried his journal, in which he wrote his plentiful observations of the Isles of Shoals, including many sheets that contained his transcription of the parish records of the Gosport church, which he had seen on his second visit to Gosport the

Fishing for cod off Block Island. *Drawing by H.W. Elliott and Captain J.W. Collins. Courtesy of the National Oceanic and Atmospheric Administration.*

Tucke monument on Star Island. *Courtesy of Russell M. Lawson.*

previous week. "This book of the Church Records of Gosport," he wrote, "is a small folio, well bound in dark calf, and about an inch thick; the paper very stout…The book is written in a very legible hand, probably by the Rev'd Mr. Tucke. The ink is not much faded." The reputation of the Reverend John Tucke was still active among the islanders, who had learned of him from their mothers and fathers and grandmothers and grandfathers. They told of his loving concern for the inhabitants of the Isles of Shoals and his forty years of ministering to these fishermen who scarcely knew right from wrong, blinded as they were by privation and want. Hawthorne, like many inquirers before and hence, wondered about John Tucke and what courage and benevolence he possessed that allowed him to dominate the lives of the islanders so that even generations later his memory was cherished. Tucke so intrigued Hawthorne that the author transcribed three thousand words from the Gosport parish records, thereby preserving through words the memory of the Isles of Shoals during the 1800s, when Hawthorne visited, as well as the 1700s, when at a particular place in time a fisher of men lived among the fishermen and fishwives, guiding, teaching, chastising, forgiving, marrying, baptizing and burying the people of Gosport.

Postscript

The Lure of the Sea

Visitors and residents alike know that there is something about the Isles of Shoals that draws a person to them. Rocks in the sea, they are an unlikely place for romance and philosophy, and yet visiting and resident Shoalers have often produced prose and poetry that recall humans from their preoccupation with the here and now to consider the sublime and eternal. Celia Thaxter knew best this call of the Isles. It has to do with the surrounding sea, the overwhelming presence of and dominance over the lives and thoughts of the Shoalers. She knew that the sea, like humans, is at the same time in constant movement, constant change, never the same, fluctuating and rolling, reflecting the shimmering sun on the surface; but within, in the blue-green deep, is an eerie mystery of unfathomable thoughts and ancient memories. For a time it is passive, peaceful, still and calm on the surface, in the doldrums, windless, hardly stirring. Yet in a flash of anger, reflecting the dark clouds of the horizon of time and experience, the soul of the sea begins to churn, the wind skims across whitecaps that crest and dip in harmony with the thundering blows crashing from above. What stirs the passive sea to transform itself into the raging storm? What spurs such self-torment, the anxiety of the deep, massive rollers rising and falling, never still, never content, an endless cycle, a recurring nightmare?

The turmoil of the sea reflects the turmoil of the human heart. Such is the attraction of the sea, which pulls humankind across time to cross it, map it, yield its plenty, conquer it, probe its depths for answers. Man sees himself in the sea and cannot keep away from his likeness, notwithstanding the terror, danger, destruction, death and taunting mystery of the sea. The sirens

Seaweed-covered rocky shore. *Courtesy of Russell M. Lawson.*

The author exploring the Isles of Shoals. *Courtesy of Russell M. Lawson.*

that pulled ancient mariners to their destruction was the sea itself, calling out to human restlessness and the futile search for peace and contentment. The sea always promises something better, some paradise, an arcadia of fulfilled dreams and never-ending bliss. Driven by the imagination, the ongoing search for metamorphoses and transformation into something else, someone else, humans succumb to the allure of the endless horizon, the promise of eternity implied in the ceaseless waves. The sea has the mark of a primordial remnant of the creation. To be on it, to cross it, to listlessly watch it, to hunger for its depths, is to reach out to the divine, to respond to God's call, to embrace that which He made, to find bearings directing the mariner of time and place to a safe cove with a firm bottom where the anchor will hold fast, and rest and peace are found.

Bibliography

Published and Unpublished Documents

Batchellor, Albert S. ed. *Laws of New Hampshire, Provincial Period.* 3 vols. Manchester: John B. Clarke Co., 1904–1915.

Baxter, James P., ed. *Documentary History of the State of Maine.* 16 vols. Portland: Lefavor-Tower, 1907–1916.

Belknap Papers. *Collections of the Massachusetts Historical Society*. Series 5, Vols. 2 and 3. Series 6, Volume 4. Boston: Massachusetts Historical Society, 1877, 1882, 1891.

Bouton, Nathaniel, et. al. *Documents and Records Relating to the Province of New-Hampshire.* 40 vols. Concord: Jenks, 1867–1943.

Journal of Richard Mather. Boston: David Clapp, 1850.

New England Historical and Genealogical Society. "The Town Records of Gosport, New Hampshire." 1913–1914.

New Hampshire Historical Society. *The Records of the Church at Gosport.* Used by Permission.

Portsmouth Public Library. *Portsmouth Town Records*. Typescript.

Tyng, Dudley. "Account of the Isles of Shoals Massachusetts." Massachusetts Historical Society, Boston. [ca. 1800] Used by Permission.

Periodicals

Alden, Timothy. "Account of Religious Societies in Portsmouth." *Collections of the Massachusetts Historical Society*. Ser. 1. Vol. 10.

"Dedication of a Memorial to Reverend John Tucke, 1702–1773." *Portsmouth Times*. July 29, 1914.

"A Description and Historical Account of the Isles of Shoals." *Collections of the Massachusetts Historical Society*. Ser. 1. Vol. 7.

Emery, Rufus. "Isles of Shoals." *The Magazine of History*. 13(1911).

"On Star Island." *Harper's New Monthly Magazine* 63 (1881).

"Sir William Pepperrell." *Sprague's Journal of Maine History*. 7(1919).

Books

Abbot, Willis J. *American Merchant Ships and Sailors*. New York: Dodd, Mead & Company, 1902.

Adams, John P. *Drowned Valley*. Hanover, NH: University Press of New England, 1976.

Adams, Nathaniel. *Annals of Portsmouth:* Portsmouth: By the author, 1825.

Aldrich, Thomas B. *An Old Town by the Sea*. New York: Houghton Mifflin, 1893.

Atkins, Francis H. *Joseph Atkins: The Story of a Family*. Dudley Atkins, 1891.

Bailyn, Bernard. *The New England Merchants in the Seventeenth Century*. Cambridge: Harvard University Press, 1979.

Barbour, Philip. *The Three Worlds of John Smith*. Boston: Houghton Mifflin, 1964.

Belknap, Jeremy. *The History of New-Hampshire*. 3 vols. Philadelphia and Boston: Aitken, Thomas and Andrew, 1784, 1791, 1792.

Benton, Josiah H. *Warning Out in New England*. Boston: Clarke, 1911.

Bradford, William. *Of Plymouth Plantation*. New York: Putnam's, 1962.

Brewster, Charles W. *Rambles about Portsmouth*. Portsmouth: By the author, 1859.

Bussey, Lawrence T. "Community, Morality and Religion on the Isles of Shoals, 1732–1773." Master's Thesis: University of New Hampshire, 1994.

Champlain, Samuel de. *Voyages*. Kila, Montana: Kessinger Publishing, 2004.

Clark, Charles. *The Eastern Frontier: The Settlement of Northern New England, 1610–1763*. Hanover, NH: University Press of New England, 1983.

Conforti, Joseph A. *Saints and Strangers: New England in British North America*. Baltimore, MD: Johns Hopkins University Press, 2006.

Daniell, Jere R. *Colonial New Hampshire: A History*. Millwood, NY: KTO Press, 1981.

Dictionary of United States History: The New England States. 2 vols. Murietta, CA: U.S. History Publishers, 2006.

Dolph, James and Ronan Donohoe. *Around Portsmouth in the Victorian Era*. Dover, NH: Arcadia, 1997.

Drake, Samuel A. *Nooks and Corners of the New England Coast*. New York: Harper, 1875.

Duncan, Roger F. *Coastal Maine: A Maritime History*. Woodstock, VT. Countryman Press, 1992.

Fairchild, Byron. *Messrs. William Pepperrell: Merchants of Piscataqua*. Ithaca, NY: Cornell University Press, 1954.

Feintuck, Burt and David H. Waters, eds. *The Encyclopedia of New England.* New Haven, CT: Yale University Press, 2005.

Fields, Annie. *Authors & Friends.* Cambridge: Houghton Mifflin, 1896.

Hosmer, James K. ed. *Winthrop's Journal: "History of New England," 1630–1649.* 2 vols. New York: Charles Scribner's Sons, 1908

Hubbard, William. "General History of New England" in *Collections of the Massachusetts Historical Society.* Series 2, Volumes 5 & 6. Boston: Massachusetts Historical Society, 1815; reprint edition. New York: Johnson Reprint Corp., 1968.

Jenness, John S. *The Isles of Shoals: An Historical Sketch.* New York: Hurd and Houghton, 1873.

Jewett, Sarah Orne. *The Poems of Celia Thaxter.* New York: Houghton, Mifflin and Co., 1896.

Josselyn, John. *New-Englands Rarities Discovered.* London: G. Widdowes, 1672.

Knoblock, Glenn A. *Historic Burial Grounds of the New Hampshire Seacoast.* Charleston, SC: Arcadia, 1999.

Labaree, Benjamin W. *Patriots and Partisans: The Merchants of Newburyport, 1764–1815.* New York: Norton, 1975.

Lawson, Russell M. *The American Plutarch: Jeremy Belknap and the Historian's Dialogue with the Past.* Westport, CT: Praeger, 1998.

______________. *On the Road Histories: New Hampshire.* Northampton, MA: Interlink, 2006.

______________. *Passaconaway's Realm: Captain John Evans and the Exploration of Mount Washington.* Hanover, NH: University Press of New England, 2002.

______________. *Portsmouth: An Old Town by the Sea.* Charlestown, SC: Arcadia Publishing, 2003.

Lindholdt, Paul, ed. *John Josselyn, Colonial Traveler: A Critical Edition of Two Voyages to New-England.* Hanover, NH: University Press of New England, 1988.

Marcou, Jane Belknap. *Life of Jeremy Belknap, D. D.: The Historian of New Hampshire*. New York: Harper Brothers, 1847.

Morison, Samuel E. *The European Discovery of America: The Northern Voyages*. New York: Oxford University Press, 1971.

Pearson, Helen, and Harold H. Bennett. *Vignettes of Portsmouth*. Portsmouth, NH: By the authors, 1913.

Preston, Richard A. *Gorges of Plymouth Fort*. Toronto: University of Toronto Press, 1953.

Russell, Howard. *Indian New England before the Mayflower*. Hanover: University Press of New England, 1980.

Saltonstall, William G. *Ports of Piscataqua*. New York: Russell, 1968.

Shipton, Clifford K. *Biographical Sketches of Those Who Attended Harvard College*. vols. 7 and 14. Boston: Massachusetts Historical Society, 1970.

Smith, John. *The Complete Works of Captain John Smith*. Edited by Philip Barbour. 3 vols. Chapel Hill: University of North Carolina Press, 1986.

Stearns, Frank P. *Sketches from Concord and Appledore*. New York: Putnams, 1895.

Tallman, Louise H. *Some of the Families of Gosport at the Isles of Shoals, 1715–1876*. Unpublished manuscript, Portsmouth Public Library, 1969.

Thaxter, Celia Laighton. *Among the Isles of Shoals*. Boston: James Osgood and Co., 1873.

Thomas, Matthew. *Rockingham County*. Augusta, ME: Alan Sutton, 1994.

Van Deventer, David. *The Emergence of Provincial New Hampshire, 1623–1741*. Baltimore: Johns Hopkins, 1976.

Varrell, William. *Rye and Rye Beach*. Dover, NH: Arcadia Publishing, 1995.

Warren, William T. and Constance S. *Then & Now: Portsmouth*. Charleston, SC: Arcadia, 2001.

Whittaker, Robert H. *Land of Lost Content: The Piscataqua River Basin and the Isles of Shoals. The People. Their Dreams. Their History*. Dover: Alan Sutton, 1993.

Williamson, William D. *The History of the State of Maine*. Hallowell, ME: Glazier, Masters, 1832.

Websites

American Lighthouse Foundation. http://www.lighthousefoundation.org.

Maine Historical Society. http://mainehistory.org/.

Maine Memory Network. http://mainememory.net.

Portsmouth Naval Shipyard. http://www.ports.navy.mil/.

Seacoast New Hampshire. http://www.seacoastnh.com.

About the Author

Russell M. Lawson lived in New Hampshire for nine years and spent six of those years in the Portsmouth area. The author of numerous books and scholarly articles, he has taught history at the University of New Hampshire, Plymouth State, Merrimack College, College of St. Joseph, Bradford College and Northern Essex. Dr. Lawson currently resides in Oklahoma, where he is the associate professor of history at Bacone College.

Also by this Author

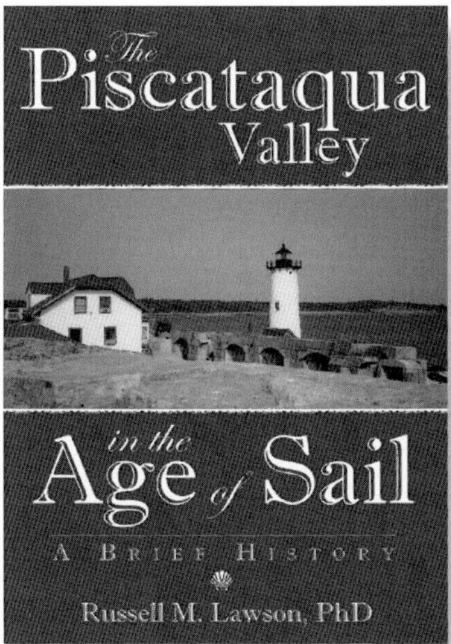

The Piscataqua Valley in the Age of Sail
A Brief History

978-1-59629-219-2 * $21.99 * May 2007

In this dynamic history, Russell M. Lawson navigates the story of the Piscataqua Valley, from 1603 through the turbulent colonial eras of the Indian Wars and the American Revolution, and into the smooth sailing of the nineteenth-century shipbuilding industry. In Dover, Durham, Exeter and the entire valley, Piscataqua played a leading role in the founding of the United States.